SAS

THE ULTIMATE WARRIORS

SAS

THE ULTIMATE WARRIORS

BROWN
BOOKS

This edition published by Brown Books
255-257 Liverpool Road
London N1 1LX

ISBN: 1-897884-21-4

This material has previously appeared as part of the reference set 'SAS'.

Produced by Brown Packaging Books Ltd
255-257 Liverpool Road
London N1 1LX

Printed in Italy

Picture Credits
Military Picture Library: front cover, 2-3, 6, 14, 22, 30, 38, 46, 144

CONTENTS

SCUD HUNTING

Saddam's Scuds were threatening to blow the UN Coalition apart. So the SAS was sent into Iraq to destroy them.

Above: Deep inside Iraqi territory, a heavily armed SAS Land Rover and its crew struggle across a flooded valley. The poor weather did not stop the SAS finding and destroying the Scud missiles.

On 20 January 1991, four SAS mobile fighting columns left their desert base at Al Jouf in western Saudi Arabia and headed for Iraq. Their mission was to find and destroy enemy Scud missiles. The Gulf War was three days old. The United Nations (UN) air campaign had achieved total air superiority and everything appeared to be going to plan. However, Saddam Hussein had an ace up his sleeve: his mobile Scuds. From inside Iraq his Scud teams fired their missiles at Israel. The Jewish state threatened retaliation. If it attacked Iraq, the UN Coalition would fall apart. General Schwarzkopf, the UN Commander-in-Chief, therefore ordered the SAS's commander, Colonel Massey, to send his men into Iraq to destroy the Scuds.

SAS Gulf War Land Rovers

The SAS Land Rover columns, two from A Squadron, two from D Squadron, headed for western Iraq, where satellites and aerial photographs had shown the Scuds were being launched. The Land Rovers themselves had been specially modified, as a member of D Squadron relates: 'A fleet of new Land Rovers arrived for us from the UK, all stripped down for desert operations and decorated with a host of weapon mounts and additional fittings.'

The SAS's orders were: search out the Scuds and radio in air attacks to knock them out. In any contacts hit hard and get out fast. In enemy territory no one has time to hang around.

Each SAS fighting column had its own search area inside Iraq. In this way there would be no 'friendly fire' incidents. Each column was made up of 12 Land Rovers and at least two motorcycle outriders. The motorcycles were the eyes and ears of the Land Rovers, scouting ahead. The Land Rovers themselves were armed with machine guns, Milan anti-tank missiles, Mark 19 automatic grenade launchers and Stinger surface-to-air missiles.

The borders between Iraq and Kuwait, both formerly part of the Ottoman Empire, have always been ill-defined. In addition, Iraq has periodically attempted to reclaim Kuwait as a lost province and to return to the situation that existed, according to the Iraqis at least, under the Ottoman Turks. After World War I Iraq and Kuwait came under British protection. The British tried to solve the border problem, but the subsequent Uqair Protocol of 1922 failed to define Kuwait's northern border. The establishment of an Arab nationalist government in Baghdad in 1958 increased tensions, but the deployment of British troops to Kuwait deterred an Iraqi invasion in 1961.

The immediate cause of the 1991 Iraqi invasion of Kuwait stemmed from the refusal of the Kuwaitis to defer the $65 billion debt Iraq owed her. In addition, Iraq believed that Kuwait was extracting oil from the Rumaila oilfield, which lay in a disputed area of territory between the two states. Iraq was also attracted to Kuwait's massive financial reserves, which could obviously alleviate the $80 billion debt she owed as a result of fighting the eight-year Iran-Iraq War and which she was finding very hard to service due to falling oil prices.

Above: Iraqi military vehicles on the streets of Kuwait City after Saddam Hussein's invasion. The tiny Kuwaiti Army fought well, but was hopelessly outnumbered by over 100,000 Iraqis.

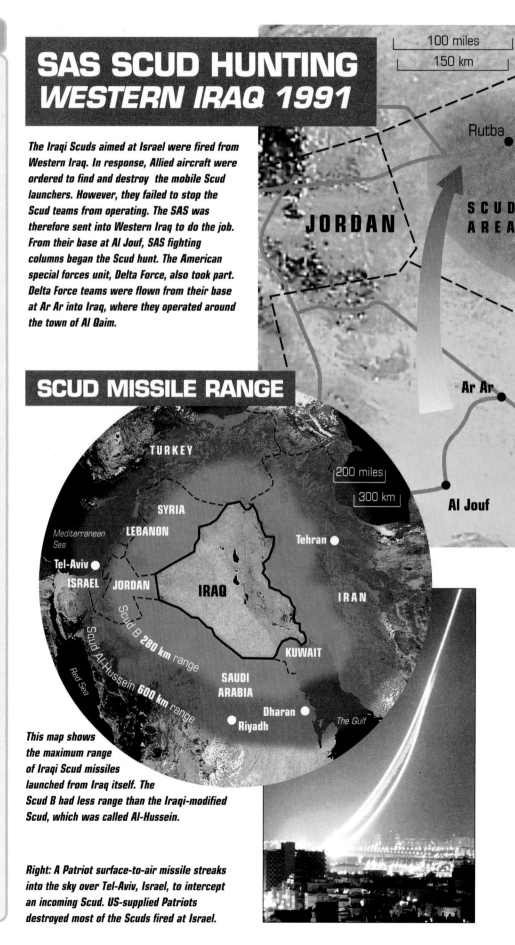

SAS SCUD HUNTING
WESTERN IRAQ 1991

100 miles
150 km

The Iraqi Scuds aimed at Israel were fired from Western Iraq. In response, Allied aircraft were ordered to find and destroy the mobile Scud launchers. However, they failed to stop the Scud teams from operating. The SAS was therefore sent into Western Iraq to do the job. From their base at Al Jouf, SAS fighting columns began the Scud hunt. The American special forces unit, Delta Force, also took part. Delta Force teams were flown from their base at Ar Ar into Iraq, where they operated around the town of Al Qaim.

Rutba

JORDAN

SCUD AREA

Ar Ar

Al Jouf

SCUD MISSILE RANGE

TURKEY

200 miles
300 km

SYRIA

Mediterranean Sea

LEBANON

Tehran

Tel-Aviv

ISRAEL

JORDAN

IRAQ

IRAN

Scud B 280 km range

Scud Al-Hussein 600 km range

Red Sea

KUWAIT

SAUDI ARABIA

Dharan

The Gulf

Riyadh

This map shows the maximum range of Iraqi Scud missiles launched from Iraq itself. The Scud B had less range than the Iraqi-modified Scud, which was called Al-Hussein.

Right: A Patriot surface-to-air missile streaks into the sky over Tel-Aviv, Israel, to intercept an incoming Scud. US-supplied Patriots destroyed most of the Scuds fired at Israel.

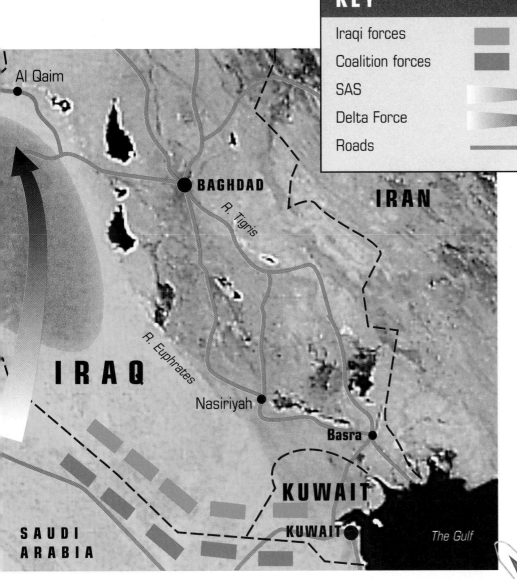

KEY

Iraqi forces	
Coalition forces	
SAS	
Delta Force	
Roads	

It was cold and wet in western Iraq in January 1991: 'We wore desert combats, but on their own they were no match for the terrible conditions. So, Goretex jackets, climbing jumpers, gloves, arctic smocks and woolly hats were pulled out of our bergens for warmth. Forget the idea of a smartly dressed patrol, we looked like a bunch of unshaven gypsies.' However, in the wet, at least the Land Rovers wouldn't kick up vast clouds of tell-tale dust as they travelled across the desert.

Stealthy approach

Some 1000m from the enemy convoy the SAS halted. Through binoculars the SAS commander scanned the scene. The Iraqis were parked by the side of the road. There were two Scud launchers, each with its missile ready to fire. Other vehicles included three trucks and two armoured personnel carriers. There were no guards, no camouflage netting. They were not expecting visitors.

The SAS procedure was simple: radio Allied headquarters in Riyadh to request an immediate air strike. HQ would then contact an AWACs aircraft, which would

The SAS soldiers were nervous about air attacks. They had been told that there were no Iraqi aircraft flying, but they were sceptical. The terrain was open and mostly flat. The vehicles could be seen for miles: 'we stood out like turds on a billiard table'. If they were spotted, they would be sitting ducks.

The first sighting

The first few days were frustrating. No sign of enemy aircraft, but no sign of Scuds either. Then, on 29 January, bingo! Captain 'A' and his column were some 100km (62 miles) inside Iraq when one of his outriders came racing back with news that a Scud convoy was near. The captain gave his orders, and the Land Rovers deployed into line and advanced towards the Scuds. There were three men on each vehicle: a driver and two gunners. The gunners flicked off the safety catches on their machine guns.

IRAQI SCUD LAUNCHER

SPECIFICATIONS

Range	180km (112 miles)
Launch weight	6370kg (14,043lb)
Crew	three
Speed	50km/hr (31mph)
Engine	6000cc
Armament	None

The SAS in the Gulf was part of the UK Special Forces Group, which was just one of the special forces formations in the Gulf. Other UN contingents had their own elite teams. The first task earmarked for the SAS was the rescue of Western

Above: Syrian special forces, just one of the elite units in the Gulf.

hostages being held as 'human shields' by the Iraqis at several sites throughout Iraq. The Regiment put together a contingency plan for the rescue of the hostages, which involved heliborne assaults against the targets where it was thought the hostages were being held.

The release of the hostages before the war started meant that for a while the SAS had no definite role.

However, the commander of UK forces in the Gulf, Lieutenant-General Peter de la Billière, decided that the Regiment should carry out reconnaissance and intelligence-gathering behind enemy lines. The hunt for Scuds was well down the list.

came screaming in low from the south. The missiles were still on their launchers. The aircraft strafed the Iraqi vehicles. Then the two aircraft circled lazily above, their pilots scanning the scene. The two Scud launchers had been destroyed. Time to leave: 'We roared off at full speed, our minds racing with thoughts of what any surviving Iraqi commander might do. We are trained to think like the enemy so we can take effective evasive action.'

More Scud kills

Earlier the same day, in a different sector, another SAS column had also spotted a Scud convoy, and it too had been destroyed by F-15s. It was not all one-way traffic, though: the enemy also had patrols out.

Later that day a third SAS fighting column was attacked by Iraqis. They appeared out of nowhere; the first the

direct available aircraft on to the target. The captain gave the coordinates using his Global Positioning System (GPS) unit, which worked via satellites orbiting the earth. It gave the user his exact position anywhere on earth. Just switch it on, press a key and the precise coordinates would flash up on screen.

The SAS vehicles were well spaced, at least 50m apart, as a precaution against attack. It takes at least an hour to launch a Scud missile; to aim it, load the fuel and make the pre-flight checks. The SAS captain hoped they had arrived in time. Some 10 minutes later two F-15 Eagles

Above: Western Iraq, late January 1991. Two SAS motorcycle outriders in 'bandit country'. Note the M16 assault rifle each man carries.

Above: An SAS team poses for the camera during a training exercise. The weapons they are carrying are Heckler & Koch MP5 submachine guns, which means the men are almost certainly practising hostage-rescue drills.

destroyed quickly. Their 50mm main guns could turn SAS Land Rovers into burning heaps of scrap metal.

Half the Land Rovers were fitted with Milans, which were fitted to the roll bars. The SAS soldiers looked through their sights and lined the cross-hairs on the Iraqi targets. They then squeezed their triggers and the missiles streaked from their launchers. The aimers kept the cross-hairs on the targets, making small adjustments to the wire-guided rockets. The missiles slammed into their targets, the armour-piercing rounds burning through the hulls and incinerating all

Above: A British CH-47 Chinook helicopter. These aircraft were used by the SAS to transport men and supplies to its Forward Operating Base at Al Jouf, as well as into enemy territory. Note the distinctive special operations paint scheme used in the Gulf. The Chinooks used by the SAS had extra internal fuel tanks to allow them to fly deep into Iraq.

KNOW THE ENEMY

Iraq had the fourth-largest army in the world when it launched the invasion of Kuwait. With nearly one million men under arms, 5500 tanks and 400 combat aircraft, Saddam Hussein felt he could offer real resistance to any Allied attempts to take back Kuwait.

Though the majority of his troops were deployed in and around Kuwait, Saddam also had forces in western Iraq, where the SAS operated. These ranged from frontline armoured and mechanised troops equipped with tanks and infantry fighting vehicles, to local militia units. The SAS never came up against enemy tanks, but they did have to cope with infantry fighting vehicles, such as Russian-built BMPs, and armoured personnel carriers, such as BTR-60s. The BMPs were armed with a cannon and anti-tank guided missiles, and posed a grave threat to SAS foot patrols or Land Rover columns.

In general the SAS found the fighting qualities of the Iraqis to be poor. For the most part they were reservists and conscripts. As such they were no match for the toughened soldiers of the SAS.

Left: Triumphal Iraqi troops hitch a lift on a tank during the First Gulf War. In general the fighting skills of the average Iraqi soldier were poor.

SAS knew about it was when the rear Land Rover was hit by a cannon round. It blew off one of the wheels and seriously injured the rear gunner. He was dragged unconscious to another Land Rover by the other two crew members as the Iraqis closed in.

The SAS vehicles quickly turned around to face their attackers. They deployed in line and halted. The three Iraqi infantry fighting vehicles had to be

those inside. Before this happened, though, one of the Iraqi infantry fighting vehicles had hit another Land Rover. The round impacted on the engine, setting it on fire. The crew baled out just as it exploded into a red fireball.

The enemy were still advancing on the SAS. Iraqi soldiers poured out of the trucks and charged towards the Land Rovers. SAS weapon skills are the best in the world, and each man is trained not

EYEWITNESS

Contact near Nukhayb
29 January 1991

'The Iraqis came towards us, all in a line, about 50 or 60. I was front gunner in one of the Rovers. I tightened the grip on the GPMG. We open up, 3- or 5-round bursts. The Iraqis go down. It's like slow motion. There are empty shell cases flying everywhere. My heart's pounding. Keep firing! I hit an Iraqi. His chest explodes. They're not humans, only targets. I feel a light tap on my arm. I'm hit but feel no pain. The adrenalin rush is unbelievable. Keep firing! Another belt into the GPMG. I kill another, and another. My gun jams. Shit! I pick up my M16. Safety catch off. It feels light compared to the GPMG. Aim, fire, aim, fire. Elation!'

Name withheld for security reasons

The Scud hunt continued. On 3 February, an SAS scouting party near the town of Ar Rutbah spotted an enemy column of 14 vehicles, all parked and under camouflage. The Iraqis moved off. The SAS followed, at a distance, and ordered an air strike. A few minutes later the F-15s appeared and hit the column.

In for the kill

As the smoke cleared, it was obvious that only one of the launchers had been destroyed. There were still two left. The SAS commander radioed for another air strike, but was told that no aircraft were available for some time. He therefore decided to finish off the convoy himself, and gave the signal to move forward.

The SAS Land Rovers advanced towards the enemy. Seconds later Milan missiles hit their targets. The remaining Scud launchers were obliterated. However, the SAS had strayed within enemy machine-gun range. Iraqi rounds from several machine-gun nests began

bouncing off the Land Rovers and kicking up dirt around them.

SAS soldiers grabbed their machine guns and ammunition and threw themselves on to the ground behind any cover they could find. The Land Rovers were totally exposed – to stay on them meant certain death. In the fading light the two sides fought a vicious firefight. The SAS soldiers fired controlled bursts, using tracer rounds to pin-point enemy targets. Automatic machine-gun fire and heavy calibre cannon rounds swept across the barren landscape. The SAS soldiers were winning, they were killing the enemy slowly but surely. The Iraqis refused to budge, though. The SAS commander knew he and his men had to leave before enemy reinforcements arrived.

The low rumbling in the distance signalled salvation. Two more F-15s appeared out of the gloom and hit the Iraqi

to fire until he has a target. The gunners had lots of targets, and they were working overtime. Firing 3- or 5-round bursts, the GPMGs and Brownings tore into the enemy ranks. The Iraqis stopped and dived to the ground. They were pinned down, too far away to use their AK-47s effectively. Iraqis began to die where they lay, their heads and upper torsos blown apart by machine-gun rounds. Another Milan round streaked across the desert floor and slammed into one of the trucks, setting it on fire.

First blood to the SAS

The Iraqis had had enough. They pulled back, boarded their remaining trucks and fled into the distance. The ground was littered with burning vehicles and dead bodies. The SAS, too, decided not to hang around. The two damaged Land Rovers were abandoned.

At night the SAS columns rested. The vehicles were parked in a circle and camouflaged with netting. They would stay there all the next morning, only venturing out in the late afternoon. Standard operating procedures (SOPs) were simple: attack at dusk, escape in the fading light.

Right: A photo for the folks back home. The crew of an SAS Land Rover pose under a Milan launcher.

column. When the smoke cleared there were no signs of life. A relieved SAS commander gave the order to retire.

By mid-February the SAS columns had almost halted the launch of Scuds against Israel. But there was no time for congratulations. The countryside was alive with Iraqi troops, all hunting for the Western soldiers.

The SAS columns inside Iraq had done a fantastic job. But they had shot off most of their ammunition, used up nearly all their fuel, and eaten much of their food. If they were to stay inside enemy territory they needed re-supplying. No problem. The Regiment would take care of it.

From its base at Al Jouf, the SAS put together a column of four-tonne trucks and loaded them with everything the fighting columns would need. The trucks, escorted by Land Rovers and motorcycle outriders, crossed the border at dusk. For 12 hours they travelled through enemy territory, before arriving at

the rendezvous, a steep wadi 145km (90 miles) inside Iraq. Over the next 24 hours all the columns came in and re-supplied themselves.

The SAS soldiers were on the hunt once more. However, most of the Scuds had been found and knocked out. By the second half of February 1991 the SAS mobile patrols began returning to Al Jouf, secure in the knowledge that they had saved the UN Coalition.

The SAS achieved a major success in tracking down the Scuds in western Iraq, which prevented Israel entering the war. There was, though, a price in terms of blood: four SAS soldiers were killed during the conflict. The SAS's contribution was summed up by the UN Commander-in-Chief, General Schwarzkopf: 'I wish to officially commend the 22nd Special Air Service (SAS) Regiment for their totally outstanding performance of military operations during Operation "Desert Storm"... The performance of the 22nd Special Air Service (SAS) Regiment during Operation "Desert Storm" was in the highest traditions of the professional military service and in keeping with the proud history and tradition that has been established by that regiment.'

DEBRIEFING

Right: General Schwarzkopf, who was initially sceptical about elite units. The SAS's actions made him think differently.

THE GREAT SAS SERB HUNT

August 1995: Sarajevo was on its knees, and the Serbs were closing in for the kill. But the SAS was about to stop them in their tracks.

The SAS had been in Bosnia for months, silently watching Bosnian Serb artillery pound the city of Sarajevo from the surrounding hills. From camouflaged hides they reported the location of each artillery and mortar position to NATO air bases in Italy and the big guns of the UN Rapid Reaction Force on Mount Igman.

Mission task

The Serbs had been pounding the defenceless Bosnian Muslim capital for nearly four years. In August 1994, over a year before the first NATO attack, two Sabre Squadrons of 22 SAS had arrived in the Balkans to begin their work with the UN peacekeeping force

The Regiment's job was to find all Serb positions. Not easy. The country over which the Bosnian war was being fought was mountainous. In addition, the Serbs were well camouflaged in dense forest.

Once in Bosnia, the SAS teams went swiftly into action. They wanted to keep out of sight of the Serbs at all costs, so they didn't use any of the British military vehicles that were painted bright UN white. Instead, the SAS soldiers set off into hostile territory on foot.

Into enemy territory

The threat of ambush or discovery was always present. The Serbs were everywhere, and in strength. They knew the territory very well, having captured it from the Bosnian Muslims over two years before. From their bunkers and trenches on the mountain sides, the Serbs had a clear view of everything that moved in the valleys below and had clear fields of fire for their weapons. But the SAS did not want to get involved in a firefight. Their job was reconnaissance. In any case, if they were captured the political embarrassment would be enormous. So,

Above: Two members of a patrol scan ahead for any signs of the enemy. The last thing SAS teams in Bosnia wanted was to get involved in firefights with the Serbs. If that happened the British soldiers and their mission would have been compromised. The aim of elite teams is to move around without being seen.

the best way of doing their job was to stay out of sight, using their skills of camouflage and concealment to get them behind the Serb lines undetected. And for this the heavily wooded country was to prove ideal. If it could hide Serb guns, then it could certainly hide the SAS patrols.

War by stealth

The SAS four-man patrols moved quickly. They used the high ground and avoided the roads and rivers, which would be watched by the Serbs.

As they moved through the woods, patrols would walk slowly in single file,

Right: The Serbs had a stranglehold on Sarajevo. Their artillery and mortars ringed the city, and they had snipers operating on its outskirts. To break the siege NATO aircraft flying from Italian bases needed to hit Serb positions with great accuracy. They had to do this for maximum effect and to minimise casualties. The intelligence supplied by SAS teams on the ground was therefore crucial to the operation.

stopping at intervals to listen for sounds of anyone following. To make sure that the patrol was not broken up if it was ambushed or got lost, the commander would regularly designate areas and places as rendezvous points (RVs). The patrol could use these to re-group if it was forced to split up.

Once they were within range of Serb positions, the SAS patrol would approach them carefully, usually at night. They would then identify them using night imaging equipment and log down their precise location. If the SAS needed to keep watch on a Serb position for any length of time, then they would build a camouflaged observation post (OP).

Below: Serb artillery pounds Bosnian targets on the outskirts of Sarajevo.
Far right: The city of Sarajevo, which the SAS helped save in August 1995.

SAVING SARAJEVO
30 AUGUST 1995

KEY

Air bases	✈
Aircraft carriers	—
Main targets	✶
Serb-held territory	
Croat/ Bosnian-held territory	

200 miles
300 km

KEY

Main air and artillery strikes	
Serb front line	
Roads	
Mt. Igman aid route	

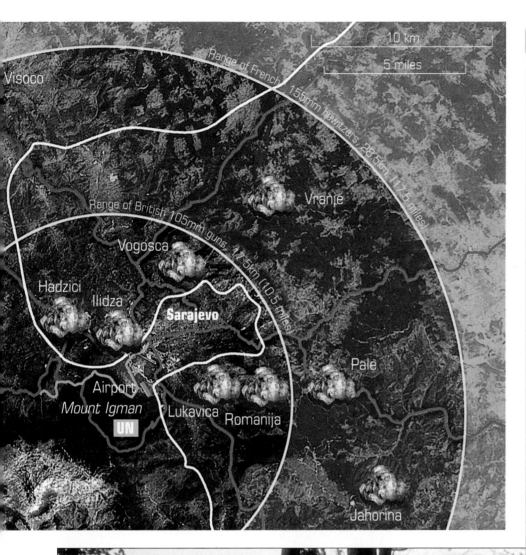

The Bosnian Serbs had been in their positions in the mountains surrounding Sarajevo for nearly 40 months, and in that time their non-stop shelling of the city had caused terrible civilian casualties. Over 10,000 innocent civilians had been killed, with a further 50,000 wounded. The United Nations (UN) had tried to stop the Serbs in May 1995 by ordering a NATO air strike, but the Serbs had responded by taking over 400 UN peacekeepers hostage. On 28 August 1995, a mortar

attack on a Sarajevo marketplace killed 38 and wounded 200, causing an international outcry. The UN decided to get tough. It threatened the Serbs with 'overwhelming force' if they did not remove their weapons from around the city. Once again the threats were ignored. On the morning of 30 August, therefore, the UN ordered in NATO aircraft against Serb targets. The SAS had been collecting intelligence about the positions of their guns and mortars. This guaranteed maximum accuracy.

Above: The commander of the Serbs around Sarajevo, General Ratko Mladic (centre). The SAS-directed air strikes reduced his heavy artillery to scrap metal, and deflated his ego somewhat.

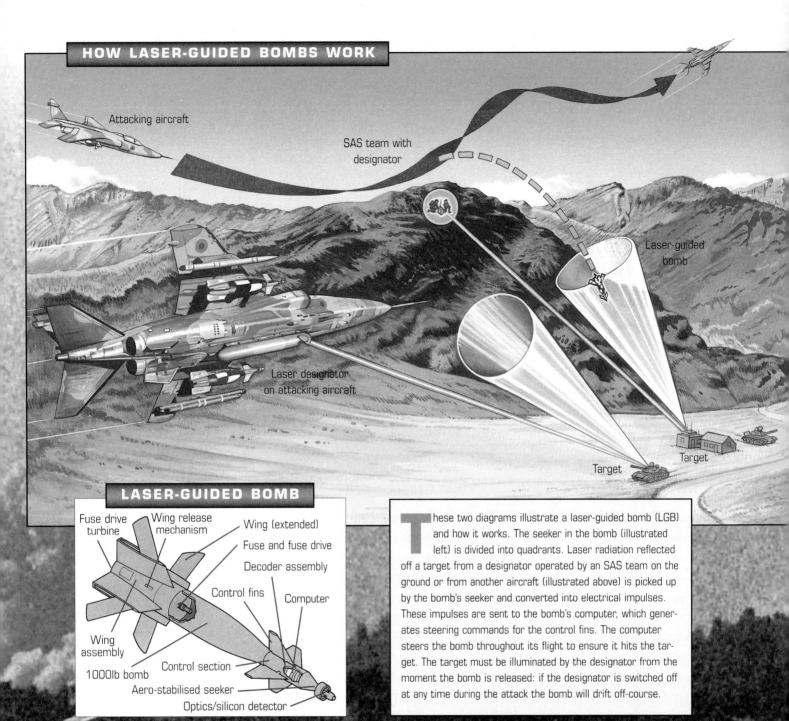

HOW LASER-GUIDED BOMBS WORK

Attacking aircraft

SAS team with designator

Laser-guided bomb

Laser designator on attacking aircraft

Target

Target

LASER-GUIDED BOMB

Fuse drive turbine

Wing release mechanism

Wing (extended)

Fuse and fuse drive

Decoder assembly

Control fins

Computer

Wing assembly

1000lb bomb

Control section

Aero-stabilised seeker

Optics/silicon detector

These two diagrams illustrate a laser-guided bomb (LGB) and how it works. The seeker in the bomb (illustrated left) is divided into quadrants. Laser radiation reflected off a target from a designator operated by an SAS team on the ground or from another aircraft (illustrated above) is picked up by the bomb's seeker and converted into electrical impulses. These impulses are sent to the bomb's computer, which generates steering commands for the control fins. The computer steers the bomb throughout its flight to ensure it hits the target. The target must be illuminated by the designator from the moment the bomb is released: if the designator is switched off at any time during the attack the bomb will drift off-course.

BRIEFING

The UN and NATO reconnaissance of Serbian army positions began in earnest in May 1995. The Allied forces recognised that the air strikes would be a political disaster if they hit civilian targets.

For this reason targeting had to be precise. The only way to ensure precision was to get men on the ground. The SAS, working with other elite units such as the French Foreign Legion, located Serb positions, especially in the UN's exclusion zone 19km (12 miles) around Sarajevo. The SAS would guide the jets, and their laser-guided bombs, on to their targets when the attacks took place.

SAS men could be living in OPs like moles for days. Lying under camouflage within sight of the Serbs, they would be unable to move during the day or make the slightest noise.

However, the Serbs were cocky. They had spent years beating the poorly armed forces of the Bosnian Government. They had the largest army in Bosnia. They had defied and humiliated the UN peacekeeping troops by taking many of them hostage. They were convinced that the West wouldn't take military action against them. They were wrong.

On 30 August 1995, just after midnight, the SAS soldiers crept towards their designated targets. When they got within visual range, it appeared that the Serbs were not taking the NATO threats of air strikes very seriously. There were no extra guards, and few of their heavy weapons were in any state of readiness.

Below: A British 105mm gun on Mount Igman opens up against Serb positions on 30 August 1995. The effectiveness of UN artillery against the Serbs was due in large part to intelligence supplied by the SAS. Many Serb mortars and guns were hit before they could be moved.

KNOW THE ENEMY

The Bosnian Serb Army under its commander, General Ratko Mladic, had been besieging the Bosnian Muslim capital Sarajevo since May 1992. Elsewhere in Bosnia, it had been responsible for the worst examples of 'ethnic cleansing', destroying over 3000 towns and villages in its attempt to carve out a 'pure' Bosnian Serb state from the remains of the former Yugoslavia. Its soldiers were for the most part poorly trained. However, a large proportion of its officers had served in the former Yugoslav Army before the outbreak of civil war and were well trained and professional. From the Yugoslav Army the Bosnian Serbs had also inherited hundreds of artillery pieces, armoured vehicles and heavy weapons. This meant they completely outgunned their opponents, the poorly armed Bosnian Muslims. Their success had made them over-confident and rather complacent. When the UN air strikes came, the Serbs showed themselves to be poorly organised.

Left: Serbian troops in Bosnia. Fighting the poorly equipped Bosnian Muslims they did well enough. However, against NATO their weaknesses were exposed.

Above: An American F-18 Hornet photographed in the sky over Sarajevo on the morning of 30 August 1995.
Above centre: The on-board video camera of a NATO jet records another Serb target being blown to pieces.
Above right: An American A-10 ground-attack aircraft returns home with empty bomb racks after giving the Serbs a bloody nose. NATO air crews were very grateful for SAS help.

At 0100 hours, the sound of jets filled the sky, and explosion after explosion rocked the air, sending great echoes of sound and flashes of brilliant light around the darkened mountains that surrounded Sarajevo. Air-raid sirens were suddenly springing up all around the city, but for once it was not the Serb guns doing the attacking. NATO jets were taking out Serbian anti-aircraft batteries and communications centres.

Retribution

The SAS men checked the time, prepared their strange, camera-like laser designators, and waited. They were close enough to their targets to remain in visual range, but far enough away to avoid being hit if one of the hi-tech bombs they were guiding dropped off course. The first air attacks destroyed the Serbians' anti-aircraft missiles and communications centres. Now the SAS men were waiting to guide in the second wave against the Serbian guns and mortars themselves.

The air raids caused chaos inside the Serb bases. By the time their gunners had their weapons ready to fire back, the second wave of NATO jets were right on top of them.

The SAS men were by now in direct radio contact with the strike aircraft, giving them precise directions as they flew towards their targets. It was a tricky time, but both the soldiers on the ground and the pilots in the air knew exactly what they were doing. They had rehearsed these complicated manoeuvres many times before.

As the pilots at last radioed that they were within bombing range, the SAS men switched on their laser designators. The designators were like large metal boxes. They sent out an invisible beam that 'lit up' their targets for the incoming Paveway bombs. Tiny lasers from the designators bounced off the Serb's weapons, creating a funnel of laser light down which the 1000lb bombs flew to score direct hits.

Shadow warriors

For over 40 minutes the air bombardment continued, with massive explosions taking place every few seconds. As the last bombs hit the Serbian lines, the SAS men were already leaving the scene. It was about 0330 hours, 30 August, and dawn was approaching. Once daylight came the British and French guns of the

DEBRIEFING

The first NATO air raids on Serb positions on 30 August 1991 came in four distinct waves, the first beginning at 0100 hours, the last ending at about 0950 hours. In all, 60 aircraft flew 200 sorties, hitting about 90 of the Serb positions targeted. The attacks did not just take place around Sarajevo. The Forward Air Controllers, many of whom were SAS soldiers, also directed the aircraft in strikes against the Serb bases at Tuzla and Gorazde. They also helped target direct hits on the Serb Army headquarters at Han Pijesak and the self-declared Bosnian Serb capital of Pale.
The raids did enormous damage to the Serb's ability to fight. However, they still would not move their weapons from around Sarajevo and so the NATO raids continued. The work of the SAS and the Forward Air Controllers continued for the next month, in which over 600 laser-guided bombs, and 400 conventional 'iron bombs', were dropped on Serb targets. By September 1995 the Serbs had begun to pull back much of their heavy equipment. The SAS had helped save Sarajevo.

UN Rapid Reaction Force would open up from the nearby heights of Mount Igman.

Back into danger

For the SAS, this successful first attack was not the end of their involvement. To see how successful the air strikes had been, NATO HQ in Italy needed detailed damage reports on the Serb positions. Air reconnaissance would not be accurate enough. Confirmation would be needed from men on the ground.

The SAS was ordered back behind Serb lines to assess the damage. After a few hours' rest the SAS teams went back into enemy territory. They had to be cautious, for now the Serbs were on full alert. If any SAS soldier was captured he would be killed. Within 24 hours, though, the SAS teams were back in UN territory, mission accomplished.

Below: Smoke rises from an ammunition depot near Pale, east of Sarajevo, 30 August 1995. The first NATO targets were ammunition sites, command centres and radar installations.

EYEWITNESS

Near Sarajevo
30 August 1995

'It's 0100 hours. I make contact with the first aircraft. He's two minutes away. I flick on the designator and light up the target – a Serb command bunker – for him. I talk to the pilot on the radio, guiding him in. I hear him approach – then he's gone. Silence. Then, Jesus! The ground rocks. The flash temporarily blinds me and my ears are ringing with the explosion. My night vision's gone. Keep thinking! Another explosion; the ground shakes. I'm covered with shit from the roof of the OP. I can't see any enemy activity. They're all dead. No, wait. Screams and shouts, then gunfire. Shit, some are still alive. Time to bug out.'

Name withheld for security reasons

MAYHEM AT MIRBAT

19 July 1972: at Mirbat in southern Oman, over 250 blood-crazed Arab guerrillas were defeated by eight SAS soldiers.

For the eight men of B Squadron, 22 SAS, the three-month tour of duty in the Omani town of Mirbat had been relatively quiet. However, the rebels, known as *adoo,* had assembled a large force in the surrounding hills. Over 250 of them waited on the Jebel Massif, all armed with AK-47 assault rifles, RPG-7 rocket grenades, light and heavy machine guns, mortars, two 75mm recoilless rifles and a Carl Gustav anti-tank rocket launcher. Their attack would take advantage of the monsoon conditions, which covered southern Dhofar in low cloud. Once the assault started, the cloud would limit the chances of the Mirbat being relieved or supported by the Sultan of Oman's Air Force (SOAF).

The lull before the storm

The defenders were in a bad way. There were only 25 Dhofar Gendarmes armed with semi-automatic FN rifles and a light machine gun in the Dhofar Gendarmerie (DG) fort. To the left of the fort and dug into a gun pit, was Mirbat's only artillery piece: a World War II-vintage 25-pounder. The only other heavy weapons in the town were located some 763m (2100ft) southwest at the SAS headquarters, known as the British Army Training

Below: The SAS 81mm mortar at Mirbat opens up against adoo (the rebels) in the days before the battle. The weapon would provide sterling service when the main attack came on 19 July.

THE

The SAS, which had operated in Oman between 1958 and 1959, were invited back in 1970 by the new Sultan Qaboos to help him cope with a rebellion by the self-proclaimed People's Front for the Liberation of the Occupied Gulf (PFLOAG). The rebel stronghold was the province of Dhofar, a remote area in the south of Oman. The SAS involvement in Oman was low-key, as the British Government was keen to deny that there were any UK troops in the country. The units were thus called British Army Training Teams. The SAS strategy in Oman reflected this, being essentially an attempt to undermine the rebels by winning over the local popu-lation. It was a classic 'hearts and minds' campaign. SAS men provided medical aid, veterinary support and began irrigation schemes. They also trained local militia units, called *firqats*, to fight the rebels.

Above: Sultan Qaboos of Oman. He over-threw his father in a coup in 1970, and introduced a civil aid programme for his people in Dhofar. This helped the SAS 'hearts and minds' campaign.

Team (BATT) house. This had an 81mm mortar beside it, plus two machine guns – a 0.5in Browning and a GPMG – mounted on its roof. The Wali's fort held 30 Askaris – Omanis from the far north of the country – armed with old bolt-action .303in rifles.

The first attack
At about 0530 hours on 19 July the *adoo* launched their attack, hitting the BATT house, town and DG fort with gunfire, rockets and bombs.

The first Captain Mike Kealy, the 23-year-old SAS commander, and his men knew of the attack was when they were woken by the mortar bombs hitting the BATT house. Reacting quickly, Kealy rolled out of his bunk, grabbed his rifle and made it up the wooden ladder to the roof. The scene that greeted him was one

of chaos. His outpost and the two forts were under heavy fire, and long lines of rebels were near-ing the barbed-wire perimeter from the north and east.

The SAS soldiers raced to their posts. Lance Corporal Peter Wignall and Corporal Roger Chapman reached the BATT house machine guns and began returning fire. At the base of the building Lance Corporal Harris manned the mor-tar, while Corporal Bob Bradshaw shout-ed down fire orders to him from the roof. Meanwhile, one of the two Fijians under Kealy's command, Corporal Labalaba, had raced across the open ground between the BATT house and the DG

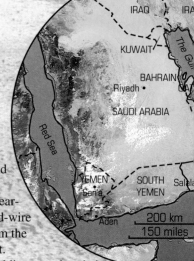

BATTLE OF MIRBAT *19 JULY 1972*

KEY

⟶ Adoo attacks
—×— Barbed wire perimeter fence
——— Route taken by Labalaba, and Savesaki
--- Route taken by Trooper Tobin and Captain Kealy
⟶ Aircraft attacks

Dhofar Gendarmie fort

Gunpit and 25-pounder gun

Wadi

SAS mortar position
SAS BATT house

Wali's fort

Mirbat

Strait of Hormuz
Musandam Peninsula
Gulf of Oman
Musqat
OMAN
Dhofar
Mirbat
Arabian Sea

Mirbat Bay

100 yards
100 metres

STRIKEMASTER STRAFING RUNS

Jebel Ali

500 metres
500 yards

SAS Reinforcements

Mirbat

Omani Strikemaster jets (inset map above) were crucial to the SAS victory at Mirbat. The first attack was conducted by two Strikemasters. The first hit rebels massing around the DG fort (No 1), while the second machine-gunned the wadi to the south (No 2). The second pair of aircraft also hit enemy troops attacking the fort (No 3), and machine-gun nests on the Jebel Ali (No 4). SAS reinforcements arrived from the south (No 5).

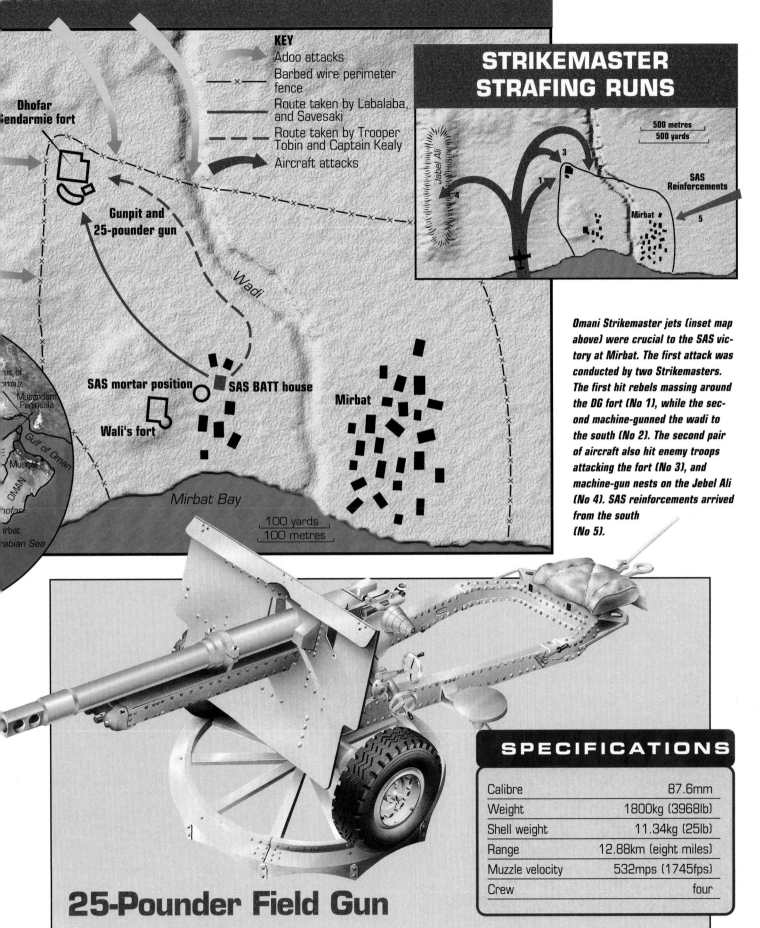

25-Pounder Field Gun

SPECIFICATIONS

Calibre	87.6mm
Weight	1800kg (3968lb)
Shell weight	11.34kg (25lb)
Range	12.88km (eight miles)
Muzzle velocity	532mps (1745fps)
Crew	four

MIRBAT TROOPER

fort to help man the 25-pounder, whose Omani gunner was in the gun pit on his own and under heavy fire.

The battle hots up

The *adoo* intensified their attacks, pouring an enormous weight of fire into the DG fort's mud walls, which seemed to disappear in a cloud of dust and debris. At the same time their assault teams of 10 or more men were closing in on the wire perimeter. At that moment the SAS men got a radio message from the gun pit. Labalaba had been hit in the chin, but was still working the gun. Trooper Savesaki, the second Fijian, took the call and asked Kealy if he could go and reinforce his countryman. Kealy agreed.

The SAS men on the BATT house roof were frantically firing at the enemy. Surrounded by piles of empty cartridge

shells, their over-heated machine-gun barrels were steaming under the monsoon rain. *Adoo* went down, their chests torn open by the machine-gun bullets. But still they kept coming.

Kealy realised he had to contact SAS headquarters at Salalah for reinforcements, otherwise he and his team would die at Mirbat. Reaching the BATT house radio, he made the call and requested an air strike as soon as possible. It was now about 0700 hours and the battle had been going on for an hour and a half.

Crisis point

The BATT house was still secure, with all the SAS men as yet uninjured, but radio contact with Labalaba and Savesaki had been lost. Also, there didn't seem to be any movement in the DG fort. If it fell, then Mirbat was lost. Someone would

Above: This SAS man at Mirbat wears desert boots without socks, olive-green trousers and belt kit. His weapon is the 7.62mm Self-Loading Rifle (SLR), the standard-issue British Army assault rifle before the introduction of the SA-80. The SLR had good range and accuracy.

Right: The BATT house, the SAS HQ at Mirbat. Below right: SAS soldiers and firqat (local militia) personnel on the outskirts of Mirbat. Before the battle the rebels had deliberately shown themselves, prompting 60 firqat to be sent to investigate and weakening the garrison. Below: The gun pit beside the DG Fort.

BRIEFING

The attack on Mirbat by the *adoo* guerrillas was meant to be an overwhelming show of force, to prove to the local populace that they were winning the war. It was also in many ways a propaganda move. Since the arrival of the SAS, the *adoo* had suffered some serious setbacks. Between September 1970 and March 1971 alone over 200 rebels had surrendered and many had been recruited by the SAS for counter-insurgency work. Mirbat was meant to stop the rot. The *adoo* planned to hold the town for a day, kill the Wali (Mayor) and his officials, then disappear back into the hills.

have to go over and find out what was going on. Kealy decided to go. He took Trooper Tobin – a trained medic – with him. Bradshaw was left in charge.

The dance with death

Using the small wadi that ran behind their position, Kealy and Tobin raced towards the gun pit. Spotted by an *adoo* machine gunner, they sprinted for their lives as rounds hit the earth all around them. They reached the gun pit and threw themselves in. The sight that greeted them was horrific.

Dead and wounded littered the ground. Labalaba, Savesaki and the Omani gunner were all badly wounded. Then there was a massive explosion and bursts of gunfire – the *adoo* attack had restarted.

Kealy and Tobin shot at the enemy with their SLR rifles, while Savesaki, despite his wound, took post on the left

KNOW THE ENEMY

The guerrillas of the People's Front for the Liberation of the Occupied Arabian Gulf (PFLOAG) were known to the SAS simply by the Arab name for enemy – *adoo*. Originally part of the nationalist Dhofar Liberation Front, they eventually came under the influence of their neighbours in Marxist South Yemen, and soon embraced the same ideology. Fortunately for the SAS strategy of counter-insurgency, the mountain tribes of Dhofar, from which most of the *adoo* came, were devoted Muslims, more interested in material wealth than political theory. Nevertheless, the *adoo* at the height of their power and popularity could count on over 2000 full-time guerrillas and nearly 3000 militia. Armed by South Yemen with Soviet and Chinese weapons, such as Kalashnikov assault rifles, RPG-7 rockets and 12.7mm machine guns, these proud mountain warriors combined their traditional fighting tactics with modern weapons to create what for a time was a dangerous insurgency in this strategically vital Gulf state. By 1970, for example, the PFLOAG had control of the whole of the Jebel Dhofar. But its hard-line communist ideology did not go down well with the locals. The PFLOAG tried to destroy the Dhofaris' tribal structure by separating children from their parents and sending them to South Yemen for

schooling in harebrained political theories. Far worse, old men were tortured for refusing to deny their God, and so-called 'people's courts' were set up on the jebel. These handed out death sentences for the most trivial of crimes. Not surprisingly, the Dhofaris began to turn against the PFLOAG. Some of the guerrillas defected to the government, and were formed into *firqat* units by the SAS training teams. Nevertheless, the PFLOAG continued to pose a serious threat in southern Oman until the war had ended in 1976, and its fighters certainly never lacked courage in battle.

Below: An adoo *fighter. His AK-47 assault rifle indicates the Soviet support the PFLOAG received in its efforts to win the war in Dhofar against the Sultan's forces.*

side of the pit. At the 25-pounder, Labalaba again went into action, loading and firing the weapon, turning the pit into a maelstrom of sound and fury. Individual *adoo* were literally blown apart, but others breached the wire.

Tragedy in the gun pit

Kealy picked off enemy soldiers with his rifle, but then Labalaba was hit and fell dead. Tobin rushed forward and took his place, but only fired a couple of rounds before he too was mortally wounded.

Kealy was now the only man in the gun pit left unharmed. He called Bradshaw at the BATT house on the radio and told him to direct the machine guns at the fort and to fire the mortar as close to the gun pit as he could.

Moments after his talk with Bradshaw, and to his horror, a grenade came over the top of the gun emplacement. Kealy braced himself for death, but the grenade failed to go off.

Just as the *adoo* closed in for the kill, two SOAF Strikemaster jets swept in from the sea, bombing and strafing them. They flew in at an altitude of less than 30m (100 feet). A relieving force of SAS troops was not far behind. As luck would have it, a group of G Squadron had just arrived in Salalah. The 23 men, after a briefing from the B Squadron commander, Major Richard Pirie, were

Above left: One of the Omani Strikemaster jets that saved the day at Mirbat. The skill and courage of the Omani pilots was extraordinary. Flying at low altitudes in cloudy conditions, their actions saved the garrison.
Below: Adoo mortar rounds land near an SAS position at Mirbat just before the battle.
Below right: An SAS sangar at Mirbat after the battle. Note the tripod-mounted GPMG.

SAS OPERATIONS IN SOUTH OMAN 1970-76

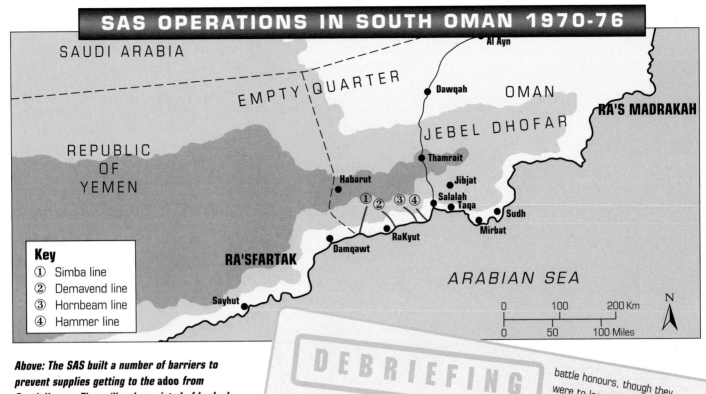

SAUDI ARABIA

EMPTY QUARTER

Al Ayn

OMAN

Dawqah

JEBEL DHOFAR

RA'S MADRAKAH

REPUBLIC
OF
YEMEN

Thamrait

Habarut

Jibjat

① ② ③ ④

Salalah
Taqa

Sudh

Mirbat

RaKyut

Damqawt

RA'SFARTAK

ARABIAN SEA

Sayhut

Key
① Simba line
② Demavend line
③ Hornbeam line
④ Hammer line

0   100   200 Km
0   50   100 Miles

N

Above: The SAS built a number of barriers to prevent supplies getting to the adoo from South Yemen. These 'lines' consisted of barbed wire, booby traps and mines.

soon on their way in three helicopters. This heavily armed force, armed with semi-automatic rifles, GPMGs and M79 grenade launchers, was soon fighting its way around the flanks of the rebels, killing as it went. The arrival of these men from G Squadron, combined with further air attacks, broke the will of the *adoo*. By 1200 hours the town had been relieved. The Battle of Mirbat was over.

DEBRIEFING

The Battle of Mirbat was to prove the turning point in the Dhofar war. The *adoo* had gambled everything on a stunning victory and failed. Their credibility had received an enormous and fatal blow. Back in their highland strongholds, the PFLOAG organisation started to fall apart as the fighters began to turn on each other in search of scapegoats. They had lost nearly 100 men as well as a great deal of materiel. For the SAS, Mirbat was to prove one of its finest battle honours, though they were to lose two men that day: the brave Fijian Labalaba and Trooper Tobin. The action at Mirbat also resulted in a number of decorations. Corporal Bradshaw received the Military Medal, while Trooper Tobin received a posthumous DCM. Labalaba received a posthumous mention in dispatches. Captain Mike Kealy himself was awarded the DSO, but tragedy was to follow him: in 1979 he died of exposure while on exercise on the Brecon Beacons. Kealy was one of the best officers to have worn an SAS beret and Winged Dagger badge, and his loss was keenly felt by the Regiment.

SIEGE BUSTERS

30 April 1980: six terrorists seize a group of hostages at the Iranian Embassy in London – the scene is set for a classic SAS hostage-rescue.

From a sixth-floor window of a block of flats overlooking the back of Princes Gate, southwest London, a group of men looked down on the roof of Number 16. A radio broke into life near-by, and a short radio message was issued to the group of black-clad SAS figures who were securing the last of their abseil ropes around the chimney stacks of the building: 'Hyde Park'.

The message was acknowledged, and the assault party of Red Team secured themselves to their ropes and prepared for the signal to drop.

At 1922 hours on 5 May 1980, the Blue Team assault party was in position in the gardens behind the building, as well as in the front rooms of Number 15.

At 1923 hours the attack signal went out to all assault teams: 'London Bridge'.

The eight soldiers of Red Team dropped off the roof towards the second-floor balcony, while the men of Blue Team rushed from the undergrowth towards the French windows on the ground-floor terrace.

Below: Operation 'Nimrod', the SAS codename for the assault on the Iranian Embassy to free the hostages, is about to begin. On the roof two members of Red Team get into position.

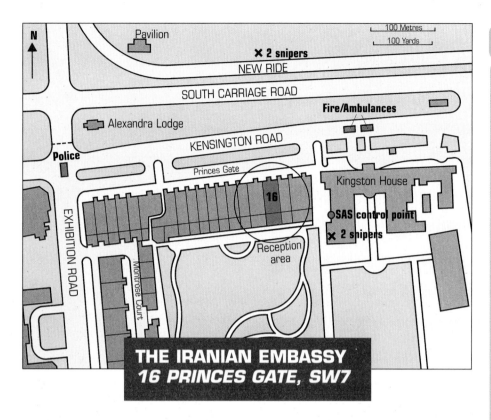

THE IRANIAN EMBASSY
16 PRINCES GATE, SW7

(Map labels: N · Pavilion · 2 snipers · NEW RIDE · SOUTH CARRIAGE ROAD · Fire/Ambulances · 100 Metres · 100 Yards · Alexandra Lodge · KENSINGTON ROAD · Police · Princes Gate · 16 · Kingston House · SAS control point · 2 snipers · Reception area · EXHIBITION ROAD · Montrose Court)

Then suddenly things went wrong. One of the NCOs in the abseil team got stuck 4.5m (15ft) above the balcony. As the other men of Red Team reached him, they desperately tried to free his rope, and in the tangle of ropes, bodies and kit, a boot went through a window.

'Nimrod' explodes into life
Suddenly the whole operation was in danger of discovery and failure. But the squadron commander acted fast. He screamed his orders over the radio net: 'Go! Go! Go!' Operation 'Nimrod', the codename for the SAS rescue, was on.

Red Team hit the balcony, as above them on the roof the explosive that had been lowered over the third-floor sky-light went off.

Blue team smashes its way in
On the ground-floor terrace, meanwhile, Blue Team was supposed to have gained entry by blowing in the ground-floor French windows with plastic explosive. However, the NCO from Red Team was still stuck on his abseil rope above them, and the explosive couldn't be risked. So they smashed their way in with sledge hammers.

At the front of the embassy, the roof-top explosion heralded the arrival of other members of Blue Team on the front balcony of Number 16.

On the balcony, four men from Blue Team had reached a front window which was going to be demolished by a clumsy looking charge of plastic explosive. The charge was about to be detonated when one of the team spotted a hostage, BBC man Sim Harris, staring back at them from the other side of the glass. He was told to get out of the way as the explosive blew in the window. A black-clad figure then yanked Harris out of the room and ordered him to take cover on the balcony of Number 18.

The terrorists react
Inside the building, the terrorists were caught completely by surprise, despite the assault's false start. But they still held an ace card: their hold over the lives of the hostages.

One of the Embassy staff – Abbas Lavasani – had already been killed. The other hostages had been divided up and separated. The men were placed in the Telex Room on the second floor, while the women were herded into the Cypher Room, also on the second floor.

When the diversionary explosion hit, the terrorists were scattered between the first and second floors. The terrorist

BACKGROUND

The siege of the Iranian Embassy in Princes Gate, London, began 30 April 1980. Six armed terrorists burst into the building and took 21 people hostage, including 15 Iranian Embassy staff, one British embassy employee, PC Trevor Lock, and five visitors, including BBC sound recordist Sim Harris. For six days negotiations continued and the siege went on, until the terrorists' patience snapped, and one of the hostages, Abbas Lavasani, the embassy's Press Officer, was shot.

Above: One of the hostages, the signs of strain clearly showing, conveys the terrorists' demands. Behind him is PC Trevor Lock, who had a concealed gun.

The British Government had decided not to sanction the use of the SAS until there was proof that the terrorists were killing hostages. Just before 1800 hours on 5 May, Lavasani's body was dumped on the pavement outside the embassy. Further intelligence from bugs placed in the building proved that the terrorists were planning more murders. The time for talking was over. At 1858 hours, therefore, the Home Secretary, William Whitelaw, authorised military action. At 1907 hours, the Metropolitan Police formally handed over control of the siege to the Commanding Officer of 22nd Special Air Service Regiment, Lieutenant-Colonel Michael Rose. The assault to free the hostages was about to begin.

Above: The press and public are kept well back as the SAS teams go into 16 Princes Gate. Smoke pours from the embassy as stun grenades and explosives are used.

leader, 'Awn', was in an office on the first floor front with hostage PC Trevor Lock. At the sound of the skylight blowing in, Lock pulled his own pistol, which he had concealed since the siege began, and made an attempt to shoot the terrorist, but couldn't do it in cold blood. Awn turned instantly on the policeman and a bitter struggle developed.

At the same time, the window in the office next door blew in, and Blue Team made its entrance. Running into the

building, Lance Corporal 'McD' broke into the fight, pulled Lock away and shot the terrorist.

The hunt for the hostages

On the floor above, Red Team wasn't having much luck. They had burst in from the second-floor balcony, but had found the doors in the office locked and barricaded. Also, their stun grenades had set the room on fire. Below them on the ground floor, the rest of Blue Team had made their way through the library and were now scouring the ground floor and basement for the terrorists.

Back on the first floor, the SAS gunfire had drawn a second terrorist, 'Abbas', out of the Ambassador's office at the rear. He was shot by three SAS soldiers.

For the men of Red Team, the rear office was becoming an uncomfortable

'PAGODA' TROOPER

'Pagoda' was the codename for the SAS unit that carried out the storming of the embassy. This trooper is wearing a black flameproof Nomex assault suit, over the top of which is composite body armour. The respirator allows him to breathe in a smoke-filled room. His main weapon is the Heckler & Koch MP5 submachine gun, with a High Power pistol as a backup.

place to be in. They still could not break through the barricades, despite riddling the doors with gunfire, and the room was now well ablaze.

Losing patience, one of Red Team, Tommy Palmer, decided to try and get into the office next door. Leaving the others, he moved quickly onto the adjoining window ledge. He saw one of the terrorists, later identified as 'Shai', attempting to set the room ablaze. Palmer smashed the window and tried to shoot the terrorist, but his MP5 jammed.

The moment the SAS assault began the three remaining terrorists, 'Feisal', 'Ali' and 'Makki', had rushed into the Telex room and began shooting the hostages lying on the floor. They killed one, Ali Samad-Zadeh, and severely wounded two others. As the shootings were taking place, the three gunmen were joined by

KNOW THE ENEMY

The terrorists who took the embassy were sponsored and armed by Saddam Hussein's Iraq. They were part of an obscure group known as the Democratic Revolutionary Front for the Liberation of Arabistan (a region of Iran). There were six in all: Awn Ali Mohammed (the group's leader), Shakir Abdullah Fadhil (known as 'Feisal', the group's second-in-command), Fowzi Badavi Nejad (known as 'Ali'), Makki Hounoun Alid, Ali Abdullah, and Thamir Mohamed Husein (known as 'Abbas'). They arrived in Britain at the end of March 1980, together with their Iraqi controller, who also supplied their weapons for the operation.

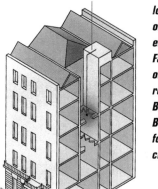

Third-floor skylight

Left: To create a diversion the SAS lowered an explosive device down onto the third-floor skylight of the embassy.
Far left: Red Team members seconds before they abseiled down the rear of the embassy.
Below: The lull before the storm – Blue Team members inch their way forward to plant the explosive charge against the balcony window.

BRIEFING

The assault teams (Blue and Red) came from B Squadron, who had just taken over counter-terrorist duties, and were codenamed 'Pagoda'. They were commanded by Major Jeremy Phipps. The first members of the squadron were in position around the embassy within hours of the siege beginning, setting up sniping positions in Hyde Park. 'Pagoda' team began preparing for a rescue the moment they arrived on the scene. They built a replica of the five-floor, 50-room building, and established a command post on the sixth floor of Kingston House, overlooking the embassy.

OPERATION 'NIMROD'

1 Operation 'Nimrod', the SAS assault to free the hostages, begins. As a diversionary explosion rips through the third-floor skylight, Red Team abseils from the roof (5). While Blue Team men gain entry to the library.

2 At the front of the building, a four-man team from Blue Team blows in the window and rescues Sim Harris.

3 PC Trevor Lock tackles the terrorist leader 'Awn'. Two SAS men kill Awn.

4 A second terrorist runs into the Ambassador's office and is killed.

5 On the second floor, Red Team gain entry into the back office. Their grenades set the room on fire.

6 A member of Red Team chases a terrorist heading for the Telex Room, which holds the male hostages.

7 Three terrorists rush into the Telex Room and begin shooting the hostages.

8 A fourth terrorist enters the room, but is shot by a pursuing SAS man.

9 The rest of Red Team burst out of the office and head for the Telex Room.

10 They discover one of the terrorists with a primed grenade and kill him.

11 The women hostages are freed from the Cypher Room and evacuated.

12 As the hostages are being led away to the first floor, one of the terrorists is spotted. He pulls a grenade and is riddled with bullets.

13 The hostages are led out to the gardens behind the building. Here the last terrorist is found, wounded but alive.

The building has been cleared. The SAS teams vanish quickly. The operation has taken just 17 minutes.

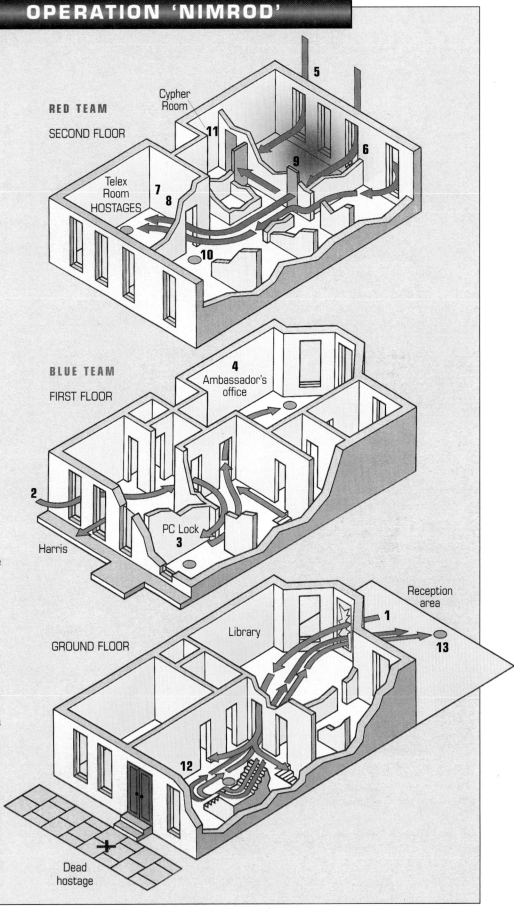

The Iranian Embassy
5 May 1980

'The eight call signs rose to their feet as one and then we were sweeping in through the splintered door. All feelings of doubt and fear had disappeared. I was blasted. The adrenalin was bursting through my bloodstream. Fearsome! I got a fearsome rush, the best one of my life. I had the heavy body armour on, with high-velocity plates front and back. During training it weighs a ton. Now it felt like a T-shirt. Search and destroy.'
Soldier 'I'

Above left: Blue Team goes in.
Right, opposite: The price of taking on the SAS – a terrorist lies dead inside the Iranian Embassy. The SAS dealt with this threat in the centre of London with lethal ferocity.

Said, who came running in from the back office with Palmer in hot pursuit.

The rest of Red Team finally broke down the doors at this moment, and, hearing the terrorists' gunfire from the Telex Room, were right behind Palmer as he kicked in the Telex Room door and killed Said with a single shot to the head.

1 *Red Team abseils down the rear of the embassy.*

2 *They gain entry, but the NCO in the top of the picture is stuck.*

3 *His comrades try to free him as flames lick around him.*

The rest of Red Team followed Palmer into the Telex Room. The dead lay among the wounded and the living, and there was no sight of the terrorists. They had thrown away their guns and squirmed their way in among their captives.

As the SAS soldiers started manhandling the hostages towards the stairs, they noticed one man, later identified as the terrorist 'Makki', making suspicious movements. He was shot and killed.

Cries from the Cypher Room led the SAS men to the women hostages, who were freed. They and the rest of the hostages were bundled into the garden, where they were all properly identified.

It was one of the women hostages who spotted the second terrorist, 'Feisal', lurking at the back of the group. As the man pulled a fragmentation grenade, the nearest SAS man, 'Trooper 'I'', hit him with the butt of his sub-machine gun. The terrorist never got a chance to recover. At least four MP5s put 39 rounds into him. The last terrorist escaped with his life and was handed over to the police.

At 1940 hours, just 17 minutes after it had begun, the operation was over.

Above: The hostages were made to lie down on the lawn at the rear. Their hands were tied – the SAS soldiers weren't taking any chances. Just as well: one of them was a terrorist!

Above: The aftermath – policemen guard the burnt-out Iranian Embassy. The rescue sent a message to terrorists that hostage-taking would not be tolerated on mainland Britain.

DEBRIEFING

At 2000 hours, Lieutenant-Colonel Michael Rose, the commander of 22 SAS, handed back control of the embassy to the Metropolitan Police, officially ending the Regiment's role in the siege. As swiftly as they had arrived, the black-clad assault teams vanished, back to Hereford or the Regent's Park Barracks where they had been billeted during the siege. The mission – played out live before the world's press and television cameras – had been a stunning success, and created a public image of the Regiment which was to last for years to come. And yet the very success of the hostage-rescue mission presented problems for the SAS. Straight away everyone wanted to know about the Regiment. For a unit that operates in secret and well away from the media spotlight, the attention was unwelcome. In addition, many serving soldiers wanted to be members of the SAS. Selection courses were suddenly inundated with volunteers, all wanting to have a go at bursting into buildings. This quickly died down, but the myths surrounding the SAS continue.

AMBUSH AT LOUGHALL

8 May 1987: the SAS blew away eight members of the IRA's East Tyrone Brigade in a spectacular ambush at Loughall.

The Royal Ulster Constabulary (RUC) station at Loughall, County Armagh, was a small post, manned by a sergeant and three constables, who only kept the station open part-time. Although in an isolated Protestant village, it was thought by the security services that this particular post was far too small to attract the attention of the Irish Republican Army (IRA). They did not, however, reckon with the bravado of the East Tyrone Brigade, whose recent mortar and bomb attacks on rural RUC posts had gone a long way in building a reputation for invincibility. As active service units went, the East Tyrone Brigade reckoned themselves to be the 'A' team. When they went after the station at Loughall in May 1987, however, they were to find that their luck was to run out in a major way.

Through a continued surveillance of the unit, the security services found out that the IRA unit was planning to attack Loughall, and through an unguarded telephone conversation by one of the IRA

Below: The Toyota van which was used by some of the IRA men at Loughall. When the SAS soldiers sprang their ambush it was riddled by rifle and machine-gun fire.

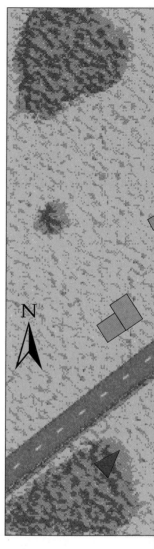

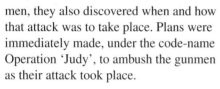

Above: The IRA men killed in the Loughall ambush. Top row, from left to right: Patrick McKearney, Tony Gormley, Jim Lynagh and Patrick Kelly. Bottom row, from left to right: Declan Arthurs, Gerard O'Callaghan, Seamus Donnelly and Eugene Kelly. For their attack on the Royal Ulster Constabulary (RUC) station at Loughall all except Donnelly wore blue boiler suits, gloves and balaclavas. Donnelly himself wore white trousers. All were hit many times by small-arms rounds.

men, they also discovered when and how that attack was to take place. Plans were immediately made, under the code-name Operation 'Judy', to ambush the gunmen as their attack took place.

SAS plans

The SAS was among the first to receive orders. The 24 men of Ulster Troop, the regular SAS contingent in the Province, were not to be the only members of the Regiment involved. Although officially the mission was designated an 'OP/React' – an Observation Post able to React – the real object of Operation 'Judy' was to spring an ambush from which there would be no escape. What was needed for the task was the superior weapons skills of the SAS, and so it was decided to send for reinforcements from Hereford. Fifteen men of G Squadron were to support the Ulster Troop, which was also to receive help from units of the Army, Ulster Defence Regiment (UDR) and Royal Ulster Constabulary (RUC).

As a location for an ambush, Loughall was ideally suited. The police post was situated away from the village and was surrounded by empty buildings – a telephone exchange and a disused barracks. To its right it was overlooked by a large

copse of trees, while directly in front – across the road – was a football field void of any cover.

The police station itself was a two-storey building surrounded by a security fence. On either side of the main gate was a low wall, while in front of the building's main entrance, a large three-sided blast wall had been built.

The SAS deploys

The SAS ambush team was divided into two main groups. The largest, under the command of a senior NCO, took post in the copse overlooking the road. This position gave the team a perfect field of fire towards the police station, and also allowed them clear fields of fire across the football field – if that was the way the terrorists chose to come.

The second SAS group was hidden inside the police station itself. This could be a very dangerous location – after all, it

was the target of the IRA gunmen and it was known that they intended to bomb the building. The SAS team, however, realised that the terrorists would have to deliver their bomb through the main gate – there was nowhere else they could gain access – so the men took up positions at the end furthest away, as well as behind the blast wall at the front entrance. In this way they had about as much protection as they could get, while still having clear fields of fire across the road.

Waiting for the terrorists

As backup to these two teams, there were also two cut-off groups to block any attempted escape, together with another SAS team which was located around the nearby Loughall Church.

Unaware of the reception that awaited them, the terrorists had travelled to the town of Dungannon, about 25 minutes drive from Loughall, where they hijacked

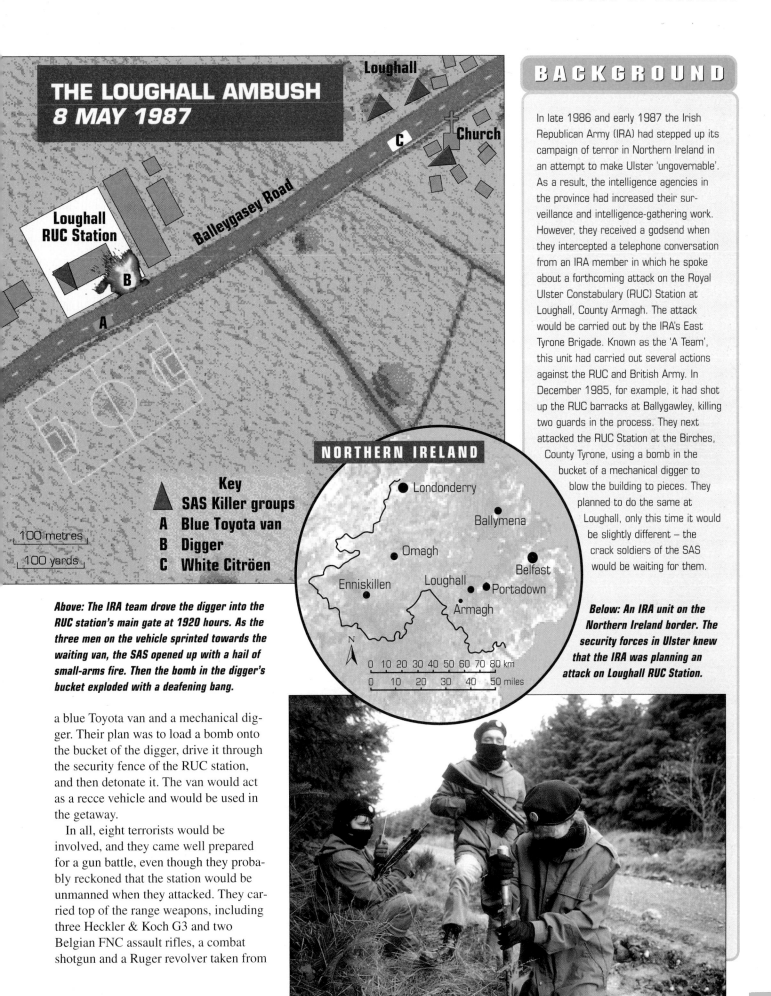

THE LOUGHALL AMBUSH
8 MAY 1987

Loughall

C

Church

**Loughall
RUC Station**

Balleygasey Road

B

A

Key
▲ **SAS Killer groups**
A Blue Toyota van
B Digger
C White Citröen

100 metres
100 yards

NORTHERN IRELAND

Londonderry

Ballymena

Omagh

Loughall   Belfast

Enniskillen   Portadown

Armagh

N

0 10 20 30 40 50 60 70 80 km
0   10   20   30   40   50 miles

BACKGROUND

In late 1986 and early 1987 the Irish Republican Army (IRA) had stepped up its campaign of terror in Northern Ireland in an attempt to make Ulster 'ungovernable'. As a result, the intelligence agencies in the province had increased their surveillance and intelligence-gathering work. However, they received a godsend when they intercepted a telephone conversation from an IRA member in which he spoke about a forthcoming attack on the Royal Ulster Constabulary (RUC) Station at Loughall, County Armagh. The attack would be carried out by the IRA's East Tyrone Brigade. Known as the 'A Team', this unit had carried out several actions against the RUC and British Army. In December 1985, for example, it had shot up the RUC barracks at Ballygawley, killing two guards in the process. They next attacked the RUC Station at the Birches, County Tyrone, using a bomb in the bucket of a mechanical digger to blow the building to pieces. They planned to do the same at Loughall, only this time it would be slightly different – the crack soldiers of the SAS would be waiting for them.

Above: The IRA team drove the digger into the RUC station's main gate at 1920 hours. As the three men on the vehicle sprinted towards the waiting van, the SAS opened up with a hail of small-arms fire. Then the bomb in the digger's bucket exploded with a deafening bang.

Below: An IRA unit on the Northern Ireland border. The security forces in Ulster knew that the IRA was planning an attack on Loughall RUC Station.

a blue Toyota van and a mechanical digger. Their plan was to load a bomb onto the bucket of the digger, drive it through the security fence of the RUC station, and then detonate it. The van would act as a recce vehicle and would be used in the getaway.

In all, eight terrorists would be involved, and they came well prepared for a gun battle, even though they probably reckoned that the station would be unmanned when they attacked. They carried top of the range weapons, including three Heckler & Koch G3 and two Belgian FNC assault rifles, a combat shotgun and a Ruger revolver taken from

Above: An aerial photograph of Loughall RUC Station after the ambush. Note the damage to the building and the charred wreck of the digger. SAS soldiers were deployed in the police station itself, though they were towards the rear of the building.

KNOW THE ENEMY

The Irish Republican Army (IRA) has been in existence since 1919, but the modern-day terrorists bear little resemblance to their predecessors. Despite the ceasefire that came into effect towards the end of 1994, the IRA still has a core of gunmen who are among the most difficult foes the SAS has ever faced. At the top of the IRA is a 12-man Army Executive which elects the seven-man Army Council. The Council dictates the IRA's military operations. The IRA's Southern and Northern Commands are in turn split into brigades, then battalions, companies and active service units (ASUs). For reasons of security there are only 50 full-time IRA 'soldiers', though there are estimated to be a further 500 volunteers who provide logistical support for military operations. Without exception the individuals of the ASUs are highly trained and motivated, and quite ruthless. A continual flow of funds from both legitimate and illegal sources means the IRA can afford to equip its fighters with the best kit.

Right: The SAS's deadliest enemy – an IRA gunman. His weapon is a Russian-built 7.62mm assault rifle.

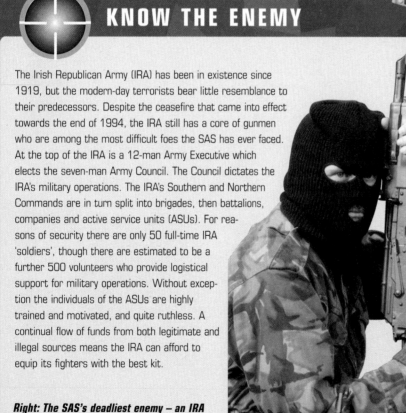

a dead RUC officer from one of their earlier 'successes'. Two of the men wore body armour, and all except one were wearing boiler suits, balaclavas and gloves. The terrorists were in high spirits as they prepared their attack.

The bomb was loaded onto the digger at an isolated farm house, and then driven to Loughall along empty country roads. The Toyota van took a more direct route, down the main Armagh road to Loughall to check whether the road was clear. The terrorists saw nothing to make them suspicious, but they were nevertheless under surveillance each step of the way.

Last moments of peace

At the ambush sites, the SAS men lying in wait at the copse and inside the RUC station listened on the radio net to the approach of the terrorists, and went through their habitual last-minute weapon checks. They were expecting the IRA men to be heavily armed, so came prepared to counter them. The men of the Ulster Troop carried H & K G3s, while the men of G Squadron were armed with

BRIEFING

The SAS plan to ambush the IRA team at Loughall was codenamed Operation 'Judy'. The men were fully briefed before they went into position in and around the police station. The commander of the SAS soldiers was a staff sergeant from the Regiment's Ulster Troop. He was an experienced commander who would ensure that the mission went according to plan. He informed the SAS soldiers that the operation was to be an OP/React – an Observation Post able to React. In the Regiment's parlance this means that it was going to be an ambush. The enemy would drive into a pre-arranged killing ground, where they would be engaged and neutralised. There were two groups covering the killing ground – in the copse and in the station – with more cut-off groups in Loughall itself.

Above: The view from the RUC station looking towards the copse where one of the SAS groups was stationed.

the favoured SAS weapon, the M16. There were also two 7.62mm GPMG machine guns which were posted in the copse, with clear arcs of fire down the road. Since the RUC station and the road were surrounded by open country, the SAS ambush teams also had backup from RUC snipers and other security patrols. These formed an outer cordon to the ambush sight to prevent any possible escape across the open fields.

The IRA attacks

Unaware of the forces ranged against them, the IRA men drove into Loughall at about 1915 hours. The van came first, passing the church on its way past the police station. The SAS team hiding there called through to the men in the ambush positions who made ready. The digger came next, the bomb hidden in the bucket by a pile of rubble. From a distance it looked like nothing more than a council vehicle on its way from a job. Until, of course, you spotted the armed man in a balaclava riding shotgun on it.

SAS SOLDIER

This member of Ulster Troop who took part in the Loughall ambush is armed with a 5.56mm M16 assault rifle. He is dressed in a camouflaged Parachute Regiment smock, Royal Marines Disruptive Pattern Material (DPM) trousers and high-leg boots. Around his waist he wears SAS '58-pattern ammunition pouches and around his neck a face veil.

The van stops

The van was approaching the police station by this time. It passed within 67m (225ft) of the main gate and began to drive up the hill towards the copse before it drew up over the kerb and stopped. It was now barely 90m (300ft) away from the SAS ambush team that lay hidden among the trees.

The digger followed closely behind the van and pulled up in front of the main gate. Two men jumped down and immediately ran towards the others. At the same time five of the terrorists leapt from the van and, levelling their assault weapons, opened up a barrage of automatic fire at the building.

If the gunmen thought they were just shooting at a couple of RUC men cowering in a half-empty building, what happened next must have given them an almighty shock. Their opening volleys were the signal for the ambush to be sprung. G3s, M16s and GPMGs all opened up the moment the terrorists started firing.

The SAS men open up

From inside the police station the SAS team fired into the three gunmen, killing one, Patrick Kelly, instantly. The other two made a run for the van, but by this time this too was under fire from the SAS men in the copse. Over a dozen rounds went through the windscreen, killing the driver, Seamus Donnelly, before he had a chance to drive off. Two terrorists made into the back of the van, but by this time it was little more than a

Below: The IRA was stunned by Loughall. It was the most serious loss to the Republican movement in 60 years. At a stroke one of its best units had been wiped out.

coffin. They died under a hail of bullets. Two more tried to take cover behind the van, but by this time it was well targeted. They too were shot down. The van was being peppered with bullets, and its thin metallic sides offered no protection from the SAS's firepower. As mentioned above, two of the terrorists were wearing body armour, but they might as well have been wearing tin foil for the good it did them.

The IRA men are cut down

As the ambush was sprung, the SAS concentrated their fire on the terrorists at the van. The two at the digger escaped just long enough to light the fuse on the bomb. The SAS in the building were expecting a much more sophisticated device, so they were powerless to prevent the explosion, which went off, obliterating the digger and sending a blast wave forward which completely demolished the right-hand end of the building, throwing masonry back 180m (200ft). Luckily the men inside had been posted in the safest place and avoided serious injury.

The killing fields

The explosion gave the last two terrorists just enough time to make a run for it. The ambush teams were quick to recover, though. One was shot as he tried to take cover behind the wall, and the other was cut down as he attempted to make it across the football field.

SAS 8, IRA 0

The whole ambush was over in minutes, and left all eight terrorists dead. With so much firepower being used in a residential area though, civilian casualties were always going to be a risk. Since no one in Loughall could be told that an ambush was going to take place – the need for security ruled this out completely – no one in the village knew what was going on. Likewise, none of the ambush team could be sure who was a terrorist and who wasn't.

Unfortunately, the SAS terrorists were not the only ones killed at Loughall. As the the ambush was being sprung, back in Loughall itself a white Citröen car carrying two brothers, Anthony and Oliver Hughes, was driving driving past the church. The SAS team there took them both for IRA men and opened fire. Anthony Hughes was killed, while Oliver Hughes survived, despite being hit at least four times. It was an unfortunate end to one of the most successful anti-terrorist operations the SAS ever carried out against the IRA, inflicting the worst defeat that organisation had suffered in 60 years.

When all the shooting had died down the area was sealed by the Army and RUC. The SAS soldiers were evacuated away from the scene in helicopters before the all-seeing eyes of the media arrived. As usual there were howls that the Loughall ambush was yet more proof that the British Army, and the SAS in particular, was operating a shoot-to-kill policy in Northern Ireland. Significantly, however, the Republican movement itself said in its statements that the men killed had accepted the risks of their actions.

The Loughall ambush was the most spectacular success of the SAS in Northern Ireland, of which the Regiment can feel justifiably proud. The best soldiers in the world had come up against the most ruthless terrorists and won.

Below: A mural dedicated to the eight IRA terrorists killed by the SAS at Loughall. The SAS regards the ambush as one of its most successful actions in Northern Ireland during its war against the IRA.

DEBRIEFING

Immediately after the ambush, the SAS soldiers were evacuated by helicopter. At the same time, other British Army and RUC units scoured the area looking for any more terrorists – there were none. The IRA was in shock: eight of its most experienced members had been killed in a single action. In the months afterwards the Republican movement was rife with rumours of a mole within its ranks. Morale plummeted, made worse by Sinn Fein's poor showing in the general election of June 1987. It received only 11 per cent of the vote. For many, the IRA reached its lowest ebb when it bombed the Remembrance Day ceremony at Enniskillen in November 1987. Many civilians died when the bomb exploded. This atrocity shocked the world as the images filled television screens and it did a lot of damage to the Republican movement.

For the SAS, Loughall was a major feather in its cap. Once again it had proved, if proof were needed, that it was the world's best when it came to the planning, preparation and execution of spectacular counter-terrorist missions.

PEBBLE ISLAND RAIDERS

14/15 May 1982: D Squadron, 22 SAS, destroy the enemy aircraft on Pebble Island in a lightning night attack.

At about 0600 hours on the morning of 14 May, the carrier HMS *Hermes* slowly turned into the wind and prepared to launch three Sea King helicopters of 846 Naval Air Squadron towards the distant Argentinian garrison on Pebble Island. On her wind-swept flat top, men of 16 and 19 Troops, D Squadron, 22 SAS, ran to board the waiting aircraft. They had been waiting for nearly two hours to start, and many of them thought the mission would be aborted: 'As we prepared our equipment and attended the first flight briefing with the boss of 846 Squadron, this guy appears. He was a stores officer, I think, and told us that we would never get off deck until the weather improved. He had a point. The wind had been blowing throughout the day, which prevented the helicopter blades being spread on the flight deck [below deck they were stowed with their blades folded].' But at last the wind had died down enough to allow a helicopter take-off. Operation 'Prelim' had begun.

Pre-raid reconnaissance

Waiting for the arrival of the Sea Kings on Pebble Island were men of D Squadron's 17 Troop (its Boat Troop), who had first landed four days before. In a remarkable journey, two four-man patrols had been helicoptered onto West Falkland, from where they had canoed across the treacherous waters of the Tamar Strait. One of the patrols had then marched at night across barren wilderness, and in a perfect example of the art of secret reconnaissance had set up an OP (Observation Point) just 1800m (6000ft) away from the Argentinian air base. Their position had been so exposed that they had been forced to leave their bergens behind when they eventually withdrew. Luckily, the Argentinian sentries had not been alert enough to spot the bulky packs, and so the SAS men had been able to continue their watch uncompromised.

The need for speed

The intelligence gathered was to prove vital to the success of the mission. The main raiding party when it landed was going to be supplied with the precise locations of their targets, and they would need every second of time that intelligence could give them. The attack had to take no more than 30 minutes. Any longer than that and

Below: A bullet-riddled Argentinian Pucara ground-attack aircraft lies wrecked on the Pebble Island airstrip following the SAS raid during the night of 14/15 May 1982. Another 10 aircraft were also destroyed.

the flying time of the helicopters on the return journey would effectively strand the waiting *Hermes* in broad daylight within range of Argentinian aircraft. So the SAS soldiers were going to have to rely on speed and firepower.

Weapons for the raid

As well as their M16s with their M203 grenade launchers, the men of the raiding party also carried GPMGs, M72 one-shot rocket launchers and demolition charges of plastic explosive. The M72 Light

Right and below: Pebble Island lies to the north of West Falkland. In May 1982, the Argentinians stationed a number of aircraft on its airstrip. These aircraft, mainly Pucara ground-attack models, would pose a threat to any British forces landing from San Carlos Water. They thus had to be destroyed by the SAS.

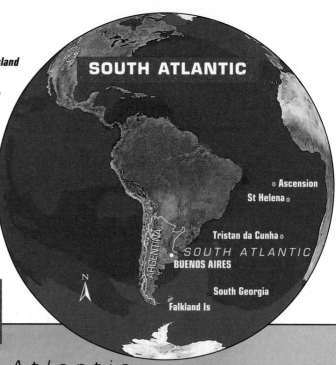

SOUTH ATLANTIC

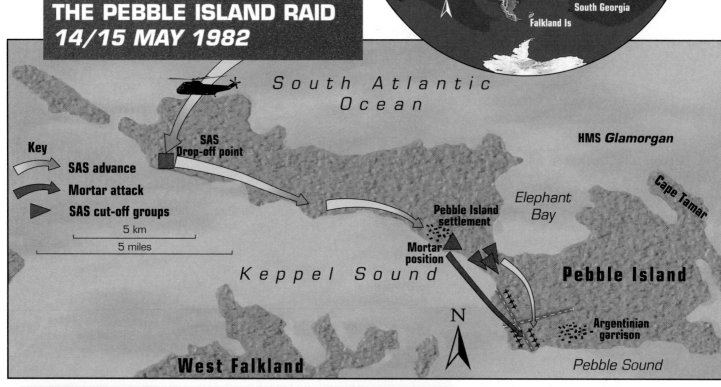

THE PEBBLE ISLAND RAID
14/15 MAY 1982

South Atlantic Ocean

SAS Drop-off point

HMS *Glamorgan*

Key

SAS advance

Mortar attack

SAS cut-off groups

5 km

5 miles

Keppel Sound

Pebble Island settlement

Elephant Bay

Cape Tamar

Mortar position

Pebble Island

West Falkland

Argentinian garrison

Pebble Sound

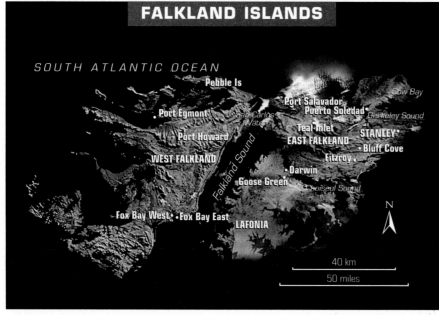

FALKLAND ISLANDS

SOUTH ATLANTIC OCEAN

Pebble Is

Port Salavador
Puerto Soledad

Cow Bay

Port Egmont

San Carlos Water

Berkeley Sound

Teal Inlet

STANLEY

Port Howard

EAST FALKLAND

Bluff Cove

WEST FALKLAND

Fitzroy

Falkland Sound

Darwin

Goose Green

Choiseul Sound

Fox Bay West   Fox Bay East

LAFONIA

40 km

50 miles

Anti-Tank Weapon (LAW) is an American throw-away rocket launcher. It is useful for SAS-type operations because it is light, which means several can be carried by one man. Because it fires a high-explosive warhead, the M72 is potent against stationary aircraft.

To give the raid fire support, each man carried two bombs for the 81mm mortar they were bringing along, and just in case the Argentinians didn't get the idea, HMS *Glamorgan*, a County Class destroyer, was moving into position north of the island to lend the attack the firepower of her two 4.5 inch guns.

At 0700 hours, after a tense 45-minute flight, the three Sea Kings touched down at the landing zone several kilometres

The Falklands War broke out on 2 April, 1982, when the forces of Argentina invaded the British colony of the Falkland Islands. The decision to send an amphibious Task Force of 10,000 men the 12,800km (8000 miles) to retake the islands was made almost immediately, and the force sailed on 5 April. Lieutenant-Colonel Michael Rose, Commanding Officer of 22 SAS, put D Squadron on standby the moment he heard of the invasion. It received its first briefing on 4 April, and an advance party of headquarters staff flew out to the forward base on Ascension Island the same day, to be followed by the rest of the squadron – 100 men – the day after. They were joined by units from the Regiment's G Squadron and Regimental HQ on 6 April. The first SAS patrols were inserted onto the Falklands on 18 April, over a month before the arrival of British troops of 3 Commando Brigade on 21 May. The Regiment's first major action of the Falklands War was the recapture of the island of South Georgia on 26 April, an operation successfully undertaken by D Squadron's Mountain Troop, together with M Company, 42 Commando, and units of the SBS.

Below: Argentinian soldiers in Stanley, the capital of the Falklands. Taking the islands was the easy bit; holding them would be much more difficult.

from the Argentinian base (in fact they were farther from the enemy than expected). After disembarking, the officers of the two attacking Troops, 16 and 19, were briefed by Captain Burls – who had been one of the Boat Troop's forward reconnaissance party.

The SAS plan

The SAS plan of attack was for 19 Troop to hit the airfield, while 16 Troop sealed off the approaches to the airfield by setting up several cut-off groups on the small spit of land which divided the two main parts of the island. Both attacking units would be guided into position by men of the Boat Troop, who would also act as a reserve and provide protection for the mortar and its crew, which was set up 4km (2.5 miles) from the Argentinian base. The naval gunfire from *Glamorgan* would be directed and controlled by Captain Chris Brown of 148 Battery Royal Artillery.

A speedy march took the 20-man attacking party of 19 Troop across bleak moorland, past the island's only civilian settlement, to a position on the north edge of the airfield. One of them remembers the ground: 'The terrain was open and bare, just as we had been told. We approached the airstrip. I could see a large house to my left, which had a line of wind-battered trees to one side. The area was riddled with fences and gates.'

Above: A group of SAS soldiers from D Squadron photographed before the Pebble Island raid. They are all armed with M16s, the Regiment's favourite assault rifle.

In front of the SAS soldiers were ranged the targets they had come so far to destroy: six Pucara and four Beech Turbo-Mentor ground-attack aircraft, plus a Skyvan transport. Alongside the aircraft were storage sheds full of the Argentinians' supply of ordnance and ammunition.

Knowing that time was against them, 19 Troop's commander, Captain John

Hamilton, ordered the attack straight away. As his men quickly advanced towards the airfield's dispersal area and the dark silhouettes of the aircraft illuminated by the moonlight, the mortar team and the guns from HMS *Glamorgan* were contacted and immediately began laying down diversionary fire on the Argentinian positions.

The battle begins

As the first air-burst shells and bombs hit their targets, Hamilton's men began raking the aircraft with gunfire and the M72s' 66mm rockets. 'The place erupted as as we opened up with our small arms and LAWs. Using three-round bursts, I emptied a magazine into a Pucara, the bullets ripping apart the nose and cockpit, sending shards of perspex into the air.'

In response the Argentinians opened up with small-arms fire, but it was ineffective. The enemy was too busy keeping his head down to make a proper job of interfering, despite the fact that the whole SAS troop was now in plain sight of the Argentinian trenches.

Surprise is total

The airfield by now was fast being lit up from end to end. Illuminating shells and mortar bombs were making target recognition easier, and in a massive explosion, one of *Glamorgan*'s 4.5 inch shells hit the airfield's fuel dump sending a massive fireball into the sky. 'By this time all the aircraft were either burning or had been riddled with bullets, their undercarriages shot away and their fuselages full of holes. In the background I heard the crump of artillery shells exploding as *Glamorgan* fired high-explosive rounds into the enemy's ammunition and fuel stores.'

The SAS soldiers, realising they now had the situation well in hand, began to systematically destroy every aircraft in sight. If the 66mm rockets didn't finish the job, then demolition

KNOW THE ENEMY

The Argentinian forces on the Falkland Islands were a mixed group. Despite the fact that most units were conscript, which were poorly led and trained, there were some units that were motivated, experienced and not overawed by the British Army. The Argentinians also had the benefit of being well-armed and close to home. Their morale, however, was to be broken by the onset of the cruel South Atlantic winter, and by the realisation that units like the SAS didn't travel half way across the world for anything less than victory.

Above: The men the SAS had to fight in the Falklands – Argentinian troops. Many were conscripts, who found the SAS professionals hard to deal with.

charges were placed under cockpits and engines to make sure. One by one the Argentinian aircraft were blown to bits.

SAS casualties

With so much ordnance going off, it was no surprise when the raiding party took its first casualty. Corporal Davey got hit in the left leg by a piece of shrapnel, but luckily medical aid was immediately to hand in the guise of Staff-Sergeant Curass,

who dressed the wound, allowing Davey to continue fighting, though he was losing blood.

Among the burning wreckage, one of the troop spotted the last remaining aircraft intact. Without hesitation, Trooper Paddy Armstrong, covered by Captain Hamilton, ran forward with a demolition charge and destroyed it. Armstrong (who would earn the nickname 'Pucara Paddy' for his exploits during the raid) was credited with destroying two aircraft

BRIEFING

Pebble Island lies to the north of West Falkland, and even by South Atlantic standards it is an isolated place. The Argentinians certainly thought so, and decided it was the ideal location to relocate some of their ground-attack aircraft, which were coming under increasing Royal Navy Sea Harrier air attack at the main Falkland air base at Port Stanley. The planned British beachhead on West Falkland could be seriously damaged by these aircraft, especially when the landings at *San Carlos Water* took place. In particular, the Argentine Pucara ground-attack aircraft would make short work of the British landing craft and trans-

Above: A Pucara ground-attack aircraft, like those stationed on Pebble Island.

port ships. It was decided, therefore, to send three troops – 45 men – of D Squadron, commanded by Major Cedric Delves, to Pebble Island to deal with both the aircraft and the Argentinian garrison of 120 soldiers.

SAS SOLDIER

Right: As protection against the bitter Falklands winter, this SAS Fijian NCO wears a civilian Gore-Tex weatherproof jacket, over which is the characteristic SAS belt equipment. His weapon is a camouflaged 7.62mm Self-Loading Rifle (SLR), although the M16/M203 combination was already in widespread use among SAS units.

Fijians saw long and distinguished service with the Regiment, particularly in the Middle East in the 1960s and 1970s. Recruitment into 22 SAS from foreign countries ended soon after the Falklands Campaign in 1982, but began again in 1995 with the acceptance of a member of the Gurkha Regiment.

Left: Sea King helicopters, similar to those used to transport D Squadron to Pebble Island, approach HMS Hermes off the Falklands.

single-handed, as was Captain Hamilton. Both men were later to die in the Falklands campaign.

The speedy withdrawal

With the last aircraft destroyed, and their fuel and ordnance in flames, 19 Troop began to regroup and withdraw. At this point they took their second casualty. Corporal Paul Bunker took the full blast of a command-detonated land mine which blew him 3m (10ft) across the airfield. Miraculously he escaped with just concussion.

It was time to leave the area as quickly as possible: 'The forward observers had done a champion job. Now they were directing the gunfire to cover our retreat. We did a quick check on the aircraft, trying to identify them all to make sure they were all disabled. When you're on a raid you don't f*** around. Time is precious. If you've achieved the element of surprise things go your way for a while. But in fact you are

Above: A Pucara aircraft, blown to pieces by charges of plastic explosive, lies on the Pebble Island airstrip following D Squadron's visit. In total the SAS destroyed 11 enemy aircraft during the raid.

very vulnerable, and for all you know there might be an enemy battalion behind the nearest hill waiting to fall on you like a ton of shit.'

It was at this point that 19 Troop made its first direct Argentinian contact. As they moved towards the Pebble Island settlement, ahead of the soldiers came the unmistakable sound of Spanish voices, at least four or five of them. Corporal Davey, despite his wound, immediately opened up with his M16 and grenades from the M203. There were screams in the darkness and then silence. The raiders moved on.

By now the men of 19 Troop, as well as all the other support units, had regrouped at the RV (rendezvous point) and were waiting for the arrival of the Sea Kings. There were no further contacts with the enemy, who all seemed to have gone to ground. At 0930 hours – right on time – the first of the helicopters made its landing, despite the fact that it had begun to blow a Force 9 gale. The two casualties were loaded first – 'We

Below: The Pebble Island raid was a textbook example of how a special forces mission should be carried out – extensive planning, thorough reconnaissance, and maximum speed and surprise for the actual assault itself.

never leave our wounded behind, it's an unwritten law in the Regiment' – swiftly followed by the rest of the units. Within minutes all the Sea Kings were making the journey back to *Hermes*. Operation 'Prelim' had been a resounding success, in the best traditions of the Regiment.

Tragic aftermath

On 19 May 1982, a Sea King helicopter transporting SAS soldiers from the carrier *Hermes* to the commando landing ship *Intrepid* inexplicably crashed into the sea. The flight was the last one of the day and contained a mixture of D and G Squadron personnel.

The helicopter took off from *Hermes* in the fading light and headed towards *Intrepid*. As it approached, the pilot was informed that there was another helicopter on the ship's flight deck and he would have to make a second pass before he could land – all straightforward stuff. Suddenly, there was a loud bang and the aircraft crashed into the freezing water. It appears that a large bird, probably an albatross or petrel, had flown into the air

intake. Whatever the cause, the pilot had insufficient height to recover control of the Sea King and it hit the water and sank within minutes. In this accident 20 SAS soldiers were killed, mostly very experienced men – a tragic and serious loss for such a small unit.

Above: A dead Argentinian soldier on Pebble Island. As well as knocking out aircraft that could have posed a grave threat to the British amphibious landings on East Falkland, the Pebble Island raid dented enemy morale. Once again the words Special Air Service had struck fear into the heart of the enemy.

DEBRIEFING

The dramatic success of the Pebble Island raid was a fine reminder of the original SAS airfield raids of World War II. For the cost of only two wounded, the men of D Squadron had destroyed 11 enemy aircraft and neutralised Pebble Island as an effective Argentinian base. From inception to final execution the entire operation took only 5 days. Admiral Woodward, leader of the Task Force, later described Operation 'Prelim' as 'easily the best example of a successful "all-arms" special operation we are likely to see in a very long while'. Argentinian morale dropped like a stone. As well as the aircraft destroyed, the enemy had also lost a large quantity of ammunition and the commander of the island's garrison had been killed. As with most special forces operations, the effect the raid had was out of all proportion to its size, and contributed towards the final British victory by demoralising the enemy. For their part, the SAS soldiers who participated in the action 'felt very pleased' with themselves. Once more the SAS had proved itself to be the best elite unit in the world.

HECKLER & KOCH MP5

HAND-HELD FURY

Compact, robust, lightweight, accurate and utterly reliable, the Heckler & Koch MP5 submachine gun is ideally suited to SAS hostage-rescue operations.

Without doubt the Heckler & Koch MP5 submachine gun and all its variants is the Rolls Royce of submachine guns. Precisely manufactured, highly accurate and with a rate of fire of 13 rounds per second, it is an ideal weapon for SAS hostage-rescue and anti-terrorist operations, fulfilling as it does all the SAS's requirements for a personal weapon for use in hostage-rescue missions. But what are those requirements?

SAS requirements

SAS hostage-rescue teams train to storm buildings, ships and aircraft to free hostages. In addition, SAS units engaged in anti-terrorist actions, such as those in Northern Ireland, often have to lay ambushes and stalk terrorists. The Regiment therefore needs a weapon that has short range, a high volume of fire, is compact and light enough to bring to bear quickly against targets who were often moving and in poor light – a tall order. But in the Heckler & Koch MP5 submachine gun the SAS has found a weapon which could do all these things.

The reasons why the MP5 is such a fine weapon are not hard to find. For example, the materials and manufacturing

processes used to make the MP5 are of the highest quality. However, the manufacturers have retained the 'keep it simple' approach with regard to parts.

Underneath the body is a pistol grip and trigger mechanism, with a tough plastic shroud underneath the barrel that acts as a foregrip. The cocking handle protrudes from the left side of the receiver and to the front of the weapon, making it very easy to operate.

Above: The MP5A2 submachine gun. It differs to the A3 version in that it has a fixed butt stop, whereas the A3 has a single metal strut stock that can be slid into the weapon to reduce the gun's overall length. Both versions weigh the same.

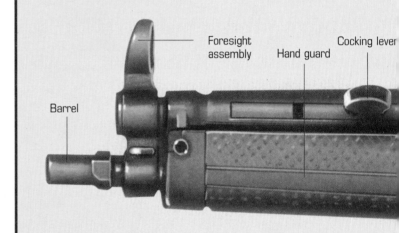

HECKLER & KOCH MP5A3

Barrel · Foresight assembly · Hand guard · Cocking lever

SPECIFICATIONS

Calibre	9mm
Weight	2.55kg (5lb 10oz)
Length	490mm (19in)
Effective range	120m (656ft)
Rate of fire	800rpm
Feed	15- or 30-round magazine
Muzzle velocity	400mps (1312fps)

The 9mm rounds are fed from either a 15- or 30-round magazine, which feeds just in front of the trigger. The MP5 has a choice of firing modes – single-shot, full-automatic or three-round burst – giving a team increased flexibility.

This combination of accuracy and firepower has made it a firm favourite with the SAS and almost all other Western anti-terrorist units. And individual SAS soldiers have had to call on the MP5's firepower on many occasions.

Left: The A3 version of the MP5 submachine gun. Here the metal stock is extended to allow aimed fire from the shoulder.

Recoil spring

Rearsight assembly

Stock (retracted)

Chambered round

Magazine

Trigger

Selector

In May 1980 the Regiment stormed the Iranian Embassy in London. The SAS soldiers were armed with MP5s. One of those who took part in the operation was Soldier 'I': 'It was as I entered the last room that I saw the dark shape crouched in the corner. Christ! This is it, I thought. We've hit the jackpot. We've found a terrorist. I jabbed my MP5 into the fire position and let off a burst of 20 rounds. There was a clang as the crouched figure crumpled and rolled over. It was a dustbin!'

Another reason for the MP5's popularity is the number of variants on offer. The A3 version, for example, has a high-quality metal strut stock which can be slid into the weapon to reduce the overall length of the gun. The MP5A3 can therefore be reduced in size from 660mm (26in) to 490mm (19in), making it ideal for shooting in

Left: In SAS hands the MP5 becomes a 9mm lead-spitting killing machine.

Right: Because it is used by the SAS, the MP5 is now the most widely used subma- chine gun with counter- terrorist units around the world.

Far right: The shortened version of the MP5, the MP5K. It has a rate of fire of 900 rounds per minute.

GOOD POINTS

✔ The Heckler & Koch MP5 is a superbly engineered weapon, making it very reliable.

✔ Its high rate of fire is very effective for putting down targets quickly in a firefight.

✔ Its three firing modes – single-shot, three-round burst and full-automatic – give SAS assault teams flexibility.

✔ The MP5's closed bolt means that the first shot is always on target – crucial in a hostage-rescue operation.

BAD POINTS

✘ Submachine guns require intensive training to shoot correctly and accurately.

✘ SAS teams need to be careful to ensure exact shot placement during a hostage-rescue, something that is often difficult with submachine guns.

✘ 30-round magazines are sometimes inadequate in an anti-terrorist firefight.

✘ In some quarters it is felt that semi-automatic pistols are better suited to hostage-rescue missions than submachine guns.

confined spaces. The MP5 is also light – 2.55kg (5lb 10 oz) empty –- which means it can be wielded with ease and even fired one-handed if required, though overall accuracy will suffer.

The MP5K (K is for kurz, meaning short) is a weapon that was specially designed for police and counter-terror- ist work, and is a shortened version designed for conceal- ment in clothing or any other confined space.

The MP5K in SAS use

The MP5K was used by the SAS in Northern Ireland dur- ing the anti-terrorist war. A typical engagement occurred on 6 December 1984, when a lone SAS soldier fought a gun battle with two Irish Republican Army (IRA) gun- men: 'I was firing automatic with my MP5K submachine gun. I fired a burst. The motorcycle kept on accelerat- ing towards me and I was forced to jump to my left to avoid being run down. I kept on firing as the motorcyclist went past me. I couldn't be

sure if I was striking him or not. During the engagement I fired a total of 30 rounds from my magazine.'

Features on the MP5K

The MP5K has a forward grip handle instead of a stock. It is mechani- cally identical to its full-sized brothers, and has a shorter barrel and a smaller 15-round magazine.

Because anti- terrorist missions are often carried out in low light or no light at all – especially when the power is cut to a building immediately prior to an SAS assault – the soldiers have to fire their submachine guns in poor light. To allow them to do this there is a wide range of optical sights avail- able for the MP5, including image intensifiers, optical sights, infrared sights and laser aiming designators (devices that put a small red dot on the target to aim at).

Though the MP5's compactness, accuracy and firepower are all important and endearing features, the two things that put it head and shoulders above its rivals are its reliability and the fact that it fires from a closed bolt.

Success with regard to hostage-rescue and counter- terrorist work – where the action is over in seconds – often comes down to reaction. Being the first to fire accu-

made of the silenced MP5. This weapon, designated MP5SD, has the same mechanism as the MP5. However, it has 30 holes drilled in its barrel, with a silencer fitted over the barrel. The silencer has two separate chambers, one of which is connected to the holes in the barrel. It serves as an expansion chamber for the propulsion gases, while the second chamber diverts the gases as they exit the muzzle. The bullet leaves the muzzle at subsonic velocity, and does not create a sonic shock wave in flight. The gun is not actually silent, but it quiet enough to make it difficult for enemy personnel to locate the firer.

rately wins the battle – the runner-up wins a place in a body bag. When an SAS team goes into action armed with MP5s, the men know they will not jam.

The MP5's closed bolt

Just as important is the closed bolt facility. Most submachine guns fire from an open bolt. This means that the bolt flies forward to chamber a round and then fires it when the trigger is pulled. This results in a shift in the gun's balance, which can mean the first shot is off target. This is not a problem in a conventional battle situation, but when an SAS team enters a room full of hostages and armed terrorists the first shot must always count (the action is over in three seconds). The chance, however slight, that a shot might be off target is one that the SAS cannot take.

First shot on target

With the MP5 there is no such problem. The weapon starts with the bolt closed. When the trigger is pulled all that happens is that the hammer is released to chamber the round – there is no balance shift and the bullet hits what it is aimed at.

Finally, mention should be

The enduring MP5

The MP5 will remain in service with the Regiment well into the next century because there is nothing around or in development that comes anywhere near it in terms of reliability, accuracy, weight and size. It is truly a great gun.

COMPETITORS

There are only two submachine guns that can be classed as rivals to the MP5.

The 9mm Uzi is reliable and compact. In addition, because of the positioning of the magazine in the pistol grip, it is easy to use in low-light conditions. Despite its small size, the Uzi is robust. Because the grip is positioned at the weapon's point of balance, it is easy to control when firing bursts. Its rate of fire of 600 rounds per minute compares favourably to the MP5's.

The Beretta M12 has a lower rate of fire than the Uzi – 550 rounds per minute – but is still a compact, robust and efficient submachine gun that is popular with Italy's special forces. It weighs in slightly heavier than the MP5 at 2.95kg (6lb 7oz).

Right: The Israeli Uzi submachine gun, a weapon that is reliable and accurate. Far right: The Italian Beretta M12, which has the bolt head recessed to go over the barrel to reduce muzzle climb.

BROWNING HIGH POWER

THE SAS'S 9MM DEATH-DEALER

For plainclothes work or hostage-rescue operations SAS soldiers need a weapon they can rely on: something that is compact but deadly – the Browning High Power fits the bill.

Compact, lightweight and easy to shoot – just three of the reasons why the Browning High Power pistol is so popular with SAS soldiers.

The High Power

Slide

Barrel

Slide stop

Chambered round

Barrel cam

Firing pin and spring

Sear

Hammer

Recoil spring and guide

Trigger

Trigger guard (two-handed)

Safety catch

Magazine follower and spring

Disconnector

Magazine release

Magazine

SPECIFICATIONS

Calibre	9mm
Weight	875g (31oz)
Length	203mm (8in)
Effective range	40m (131ft)
Rate of fire	single shot
Feed	14-round magazine
Muzzle velocity	350mps (1148fps)

The SAS uses the Browning High Power pistol mainly for hostage-rescue work and counter-terrorist operations. The two are not the same thing. Hostage-rescue, for example, involves storming terrorist-held buildings to free hostages, whereas anti-terrorism often entails SAS soldiers undertaking plainclothes work. During the conflict in Northern Ireland, for example, SAS soldiers often infiltrated staunchly Republican areas to track down Irish Republican Army (IRA) terrorists. For such work they needed reliable weapons, so they carried Browning High Power pistols. Similarly, SAS hostage-rescue teams are armed with High Powers. Why?

Pistols are designed to be fired one-handed, and they can also be brought to bear on a target more easily than a sub-machine gun or assault rifle. Also, many pistols, the High Power included, are semi-automatic. This means they fire a round every time the trigger is pulled. Some experts say that a submachine gun is better; after all, it fires full-automatic at a rate of up to 900 rounds per minute. However, the specialist weapons skills of SAS soldiers mean that the High Power becomes almost a mini submachine gun.

Firing the High Power

The High Power's magazine holds 14 rounds. SAS soldiers undergoing hostage-rescue training are taught to fire all 14

Right: The construction of the Browning High Power is extremely simple. It consists of the frame, the slide and the barrel. In an age of increasing sophistication, the High Power's simplicity is a major plus: it can be stripped and re-assembled in seconds.

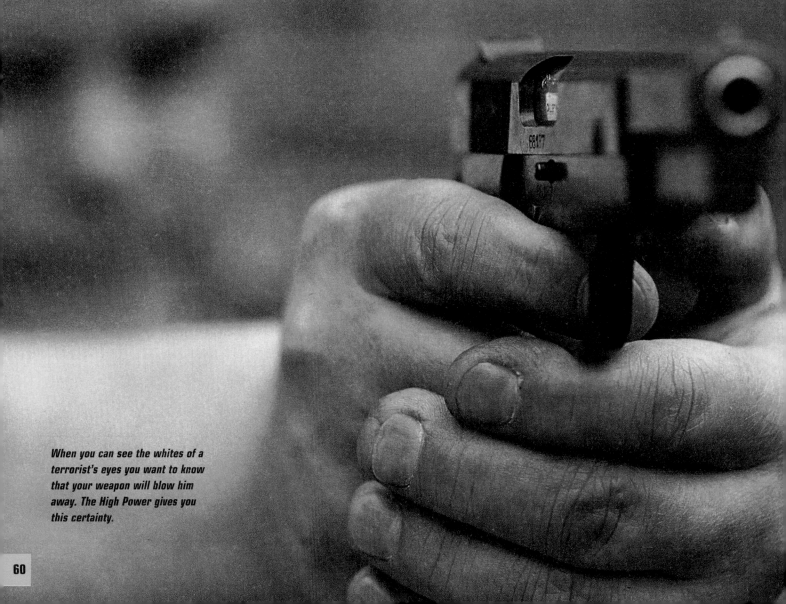

COMPETITORS

There are two makes of semi-automatic pistols that are challenging the High Power's place as the SAS's pistol.

Glock pistols (above) are very lightweight – 600g (21oz) – thanks to their receivers being made of high-resistant polymer material. This makes them ideal for hostage-rescue and covert operations. Curiously, they do not have a conventional safety catch. Safety is built into the trigger mechanism. The first squeeze of the trigger disengages the trigger safety, while the second squeeze releases the striker to fire the round.

SIG-Sauer pistols (top right), produced in Switzerland, are even more reliable than the High Power. During tests conducted by the Royal Canadian Mounted Police, for example, 10 test SIG-Sauers fired a total of 150,000 rounds. The malfunction rate was 0.007 of one per cent, an average that is even good enough for the SAS! In addition, they have magazine catches that can be reversed to provide greater convenience for left-handed users. Compact, strong and extremely accurate, SIG-Sauer pistols are major challengers to the Browning High Power.

When you can see the whites of a terrorist's eyes you want to know that your weapon will blow him away. The High Power gives you this certainty.

To the Regiment the Browning High Power is an old friend, one they will rely on well into the next century.

rounds in under three seconds – ferocious firepower. This ability for sustained firepower makes the High Power a favourite among SAS soldiers.

The requirement

The High Power fulfils all the other requirements the SAS demands of the weapons it uses for its work. These requirements are reliability (the weapon must work first time, every time – the first four seconds of a rescue are what decides the outcome), safety (there must be no risk of an accidental discharge before the assault as this will not only endanger the assault team but will also give away their approach), high-capacity magazines, compactness (very important for concealment in

---

GOOD POINTS

✔ The High Power's magazine capacity is 14 rounds, making it ideal for sustained fire.

✔ The weapon is excellent in confined spaces, such as aircraft, in a hostage-rescue.

✔ Because the trigger has to be pulled each time a round is fired, the High Power deters wild and inaccurate firing.

✔ The High Power is very reliable and accurate, two factors that are essential for anti-terrorist missions.

BAD POINTS

✘ Pistols in general have high recoils, which can reduce the accuracy of follow-on shots.

✘ The High Power, like most pistols, has only a short range, making it unsuitable for long-range firing.

✘ In certain situations a 14-round magazine is inadequate, especially against terrorists armed with submachine guns holding 30-round magazines.

✘ In some quarters it is felt that pistols are more difficult to use in hostage-rescues than submachine guns.

---

plainclothes work), rapid magazine change capacity, speedy operation and aiming. Finally, the High Power has a major advantage over its more modern and sophisticated rivals: it works even when covered in mud and grime.

The old-timer

The High Power is certainly no spring chicken – it has been in military service since 1935 – but that is one of the reasons why the Regiment uses it: it has been tried and tested in action over many decades and it works.

The latest version

The manufacturers have modified the High Power over the years, and the current version produced by FN is the Mark 3. This is a double-action High Power which has met with a favourable response from the Regiment. Double-action is a firing mechanism that allows two methods of firing. The operator can fire by manually cocking the hammer and pulling the trigger, or by cocking and releasing the hammer by placing continuous pressure on the trigger.

The fact that an SAS soldier has to pull the trigger every time he wants to fire the pistol

is also a reason why the High Power is favoured over submachine guns. It deters wild firing and encourages exact shot placement.

High power ammunition

Like most pistols, the High Power has a limited range – around 40m (131ft) – but this does not matter for close work. Targets in a hostage-rescue mission, for example, are usually engaged at ranges of 4-5m (13-16ft), sometimes nearer. This close range, however, can present problems for SAS teams. The High Power fires 9mm-calibre ammunition. The rounds have a muzzle velocity of 350mps (1148fps), substantially lower than rifle ammunition, which can be as high as 900mps (2952fps). The lower velocity means that they have less hitting power. However, because they are fired at close range they can still go through a terrorist's body and into a hostage, a problem made more likely because 9mm rounds are smooth and tapered to allow them to work efficiently in automatic weapons. Fortunately, the introduction of specialist rounds that fragment and flatten when they hit a body has alleviated this problem.

The High Power meets all the Regiment's requirements regarding weapons for hostage-rescue work, and it is likely to remain in service well into the next century. Its reliability alone is a powerful factor for its retained use with the SAS.

M16/M203 FORCE MULTIPLIER

The M16 assault rifle is an SAS soldier's best friend. Its 5.56mm rounds cut through flesh and bone with ease and, fitted with an M203 grenade launcher, it can also kill tanks.

It looks and feels like a toy. It has a plastic butt and foregrip, it weighs only 2.86kg (6.25lb) and it is only 990mm (39in) long. It makes a light popping sound when it fires instead of the loud crack of heavier assault rifles. Yet the M16, as used by the SAS, is one of the best firearms in the world.

Why do SAS soldiers like the M16? Mainly because it suits the type of mission they undertake, such as jungle operations: 'Though it doesn't have long range, it is light and compact, and is ideally suited to jungle warfare.' It is also reliable. SAS soldiers often operate in four-man teams behind enemy lines. They therefore need small arms that work first time every time. In the M16 assault rifle they have such a weapon.

The SAS has used the American M16 since its war in Borneo in the early 1960s. From the 1970s it has also used the 40mm M203 grenade launcher, which is a significant force multiplier for an SAS four-man patrol.

The M16 was originally designed by Eugene Stoner in the 1950s. He designated the weapon AR15. In 1957, it was licensed to Colt and large-scale production began. It entered service with US forces in the 1960s, under the designation M16A1.

Short-range lethality

The latest version is the M16A2, which has a new foregrip made of a stronger plastic and new firing modes. To deter wild firing it has no automatic fire capability. Instead it has a three-round burst mode.

SAS soldiers load their M16s with SS109 rounds, which are heavier and slower

The M16/M203

Labels: Carrying handle and rearsight assembly · Bolt and firing pin · Rearsight attachment · Gas tube · Fired round (being extracted) · Charging handle · Buttstock · Bolt assist · Sling swivel · Selector cam · Trigger · Grip · Sear · Hammer · Magazine · Grenade trigger

SPECIFICATIONS

Calibre	5.56mm
Weight (M16 only)	2.86kg (6.25lb)
Weight (with M203)	4.49kg (9.75lb)
Length	990mm (39in)
Effective range (M16)	400m (1312ft)
Effective range (M203)	350m (1148ft)
Rate of fire	800rpm (cyclic)
Feed	30-round magazine
Muzzle velocity	1000mps (3282fps)

Above: Hand-held fury – the M16 assault rifle and M203 grenade launcher combination. For SAS patrols these weapons are ideal. They combine firepower and reliability in one lethal package.

than the American M193 round. They give SAS M16s more stopping power. The 5.56mm round has a high lethality at close range. This means that when it hits the body it 'tumbles' and fragments, causing massive internal injuries.

Firing the M16 is easy. Because it is relatively short and light, it can be brought to bear on a target quicker than heavier assault rifles, such as the SLR. This is a major advantage in a firefight, when the first few seconds decide who wins and who loses. Because of its straightline layout (the butt, receiver and barrel are all at the same level), it has low recoil. This

means it is more comfortable to fire than larger rifles, which 'kick like a mule'.

The M16 does not have the range of 7.62mm assault rifles, but this is not a problem for SAS soldiers. They do not fight as ordinary infantrymen. Their firefights are usually conducted at short range. Overall, then, the M16 is ideally suited to SAS missions, and with an M203 grenade launcher fitted it is even better.

The M203

Hand-held grenade launchers are favoured by SAS soldiers because they can propel a projectile over a distance in excess of 300m (984ft) – the

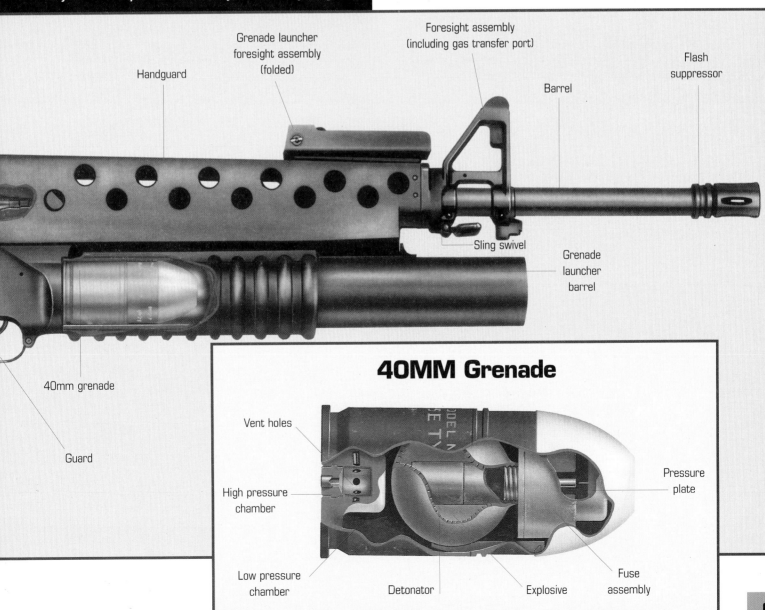

Handguard

Grenade launcher foresight assembly (folded)

Foresight assembly (including gas transfer port)

Barrel

Flash suppressor

Sling swivel

Grenade launcher barrel

40mm grenade

Guard

40MM Grenade

Vent holes

High pressure chamber

Low pressure chamber

Detonator

Explosive

Pressure plate

Fuse assembly

GOOD POINTS

✔ The M16 is lightweight compared to its 7.62mm rivals, such as the SLR.

✔ The M16, because it is compact, is easy to bring to bear in a firefight.

✔ The M203 is a significant force multiplier, which substantially increases the overall firepower of an SAS team.

✔ The M16 fires lightweight 5.56mm ammunition, which means more rounds can be carried by SAS soldiers.

BAD POINTS

✘ The M16 requires frequent cleaning to prevent fouling in the gas passages.

✘ The M16 does not stand up well to rough handling.

✘ In desert conditions, sand and grit can get into the M16's working parts, which causes stoppages.

✘ The M16 requires more cleaning than the SLR.

✘ The 5.56mm round is less lethal at ranges beyond 440m (1443ft) than the heavier 7.62mm round.

M203 itself has a range of 350m (1148ft) – which is obviously greater than a hand grenade. In addition, they can fire a variety of rounds, such as high explosive, anti-armour or anti-personnel. They are particularly useful if a unit is ambushed, as a grenade launcher can lay down a large amount of fire-power at short notice.

SAS grenade launchers

In the 1970s the SAS used the American M79 grenade launcher, a single-shot, breech-loading weapon. It was lightweight, accurate and could take a lot of punish-ment. However, it had one major disadvantage: it was a dedicated weapon. This means that the man fir-ing it carried nothing else, and was there-fore defence-less until he loaded another grenade into the breech.

In recognition of this the manufacturer came up with the M203: a 40mm single-shot grenade launcher that could be fitted under the bar-rel of the M16.

The operation of an M16 with an M203 attached is unaffected, apart from having an additional 1.63kg (3.5lb) in weight fixed. With M203s all the members of an SAS patrol could put down high-explosive suppressive fire. And they could still fire their assault rifles.

To fire the M203 the user has to pull the trigger on the

Left: Easy to bring to bear and a delight to shoot, the M16 is top of the SAS assault rifle list. It is also lighter than many 7.62mm guns – a bonus for foot patrols.

COMPETITORS

The M16 is the main SAS personal weapon in use with the Regiment. Its main competitors are the SA-80 and Steyr AUG, both of which have been tested by the SAS.

The SA-80 (below left) is easier to handle than the M16, but is thought unreliable by SAS soldiers. However, its range – 400m (1312ft) – is as good as the M16's and its accuracy is greater. In addition, it is lighter.

The Steyr AUG (below right) is an altogether better assault rifle than either the M16 or the SA-80. It has been used by SAS troopers, notably in Northern Ireland. It has excellent accuracy, optical sights, is reliable and can take a lot of punishment (much more than the M16). In addition, the AUG can be turned into anything from a submachine gun to a light support weapon by simply swapping parts. This makes it very flexible.

grenade launcher itself, which is located under the M203's chamber.

It is as a fragmentation weapon that the M203 is used by the Regiment. On Pebble Island during the 1982 Falklands War, for example, M203s were used

Above: In SAS ambushes, the M16 spews death at a rate of 800 rounds per minute.

against stationary enemy Pucara aircraft. In addition, they were also used against some of the Argentine garrison on the island.

The M203 in action

One of those who took part in the raid, Corporal Davey, D Squadron, tells the story: 'Just off the airstrip we heard Spanish voices, at least four or five, shouting some 50m [164ft] towards the settlement. I opened fire with an M203 and put down some 60 rounds [of M16 ammunition] in the direction of the voices. Two very pained screams were the only reply.'

Another who took part gave an example of the effect of the M16 and M203: 'The M203 grenades detonated on the aircraft. I clipped a fresh mag into my M16 and looked around for fresh targets. By this time the aircraft were either on fire or had been riddled with bullets.'

The M16 and M203 have been in SAS use for over 20 years, and are likely to remain in use for at least the next 20.

Below: The SAS has used the M16 and M203 in many different environments, from the deserts of Arabia to the frozen wastes of the Arctic. If properly maintained, they work whatever the weather.

SAS ATTACK LAND ROVERS

MOBILE FIREPOWER

SAS Land Rovers keep going when the going gets tough and they pack a powerful punch. Bristling with weapons, they can knock out main battle tanks and aircraft.

The SAS has used heavily armed Land Rovers since the mid-1950s. Land Rovers are light, reliable, can take a lot of punishment and can move quickly to get out of trouble. They are therefore ideal for SAS operations behind the lines.

What type of Land Rovers does the SAS use? Since 1983 the Regiment has used the coil-sprung Land Rover 110 series, called Desert Patrol Vehicles (DPVs).

After extensive trials, including evaluation of suitability for airborne, parachute and heliborne insertions, an initial batch of 32 DPVs was ordered in 1985. They were powered by the much more potent 3500cc V8 petrol engine, and had permanent

SPECIFICATIONS
General Purpose Machine Gun

Calibre	7.62mm
Weight	10.9kg (24lb)
Length	1232mm (48in)
Effective range	1800m (5904ft)
Rate of fire	750-1000rpm (cyclic)
Muzzle velocity	838mps (2748fps)

SPECIFICATIONS
Smoke Discharger

Burn time	25 seconds
Weight	2.86kg (6.25lb)
Delay time	five seconds
Effective range	30m (100ft)
Rate of fire	single shot, four canisters

SPECIFICATIONS
110 Land Rover

Powerplant	3000cc engine
Range	500km (310miles)
Maximum speed	120kmh (74mph)
Armament	machine guns, anti-tank and air-defence weapons
Drive	four-wheel drive
Gearbox	five-speed

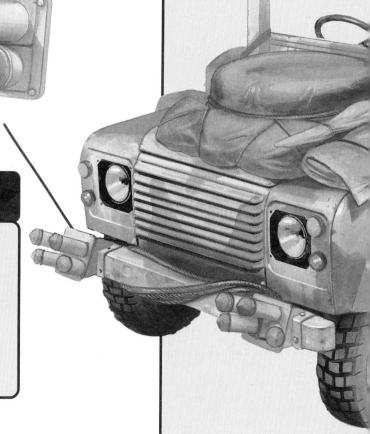

SAS 110 LAND ROVER

SPECIFICATIONS
Milan Anti-Tank Weapon

Weight (launcher only)	10kg (22lb)
Weight (missile)	6.8kg (15lb)
Length	900mm (35in)
Effective range	2000m (6560ft)
Rate of fire	single shot
Armour penetration	1060mm (41in)
Flight to max. range	12.5 seconds

SPECIFICATIONS
Mark 19 Grenade Launcher

Calibre	40mm
Weight	34kg (6.25lb)
Length	1028mm (40in)
Effective range	1600m (5248ft)
Rate of fire	325-375rpm (cyclic)
Muzzle velocity	240mps (787fps)

SPECIFICATIONS
Global Positioning System

Accuracy	to within 16m (52ft)
Weight	0.9kg (2lb)
Length	210mm (8in)
Effective range	limitless
Battery life	500 hours

Left: A fully armed and equipped SAS 110 Land Rover kitted out for desert operations. As well as the weapons shown, the vehicle carries extra firepower in the form of Stingers surface-to-air missiles (SAMs) for air defence, and M72 Light Anti-tank Weapons (LAWs). In addition, each of the three crew members are armed with personal weapons, usually M16/M203s.

COMPETITORS

Due to its compact nature and basic operational simplicity, the Land Rover has few straight competitors for special forces use. The SAS has no plans to use any other vehicle for its mobility troops. The two models below come closest to being Land Rover competitors.

The Toyota Land Cruiser (below) has had some success in the Third World. Like most Japanese vehicles, it is reliable and can take a lot of hard knocks.

The Pinzgauer (below), built by the Austrian firm Steyr-Daimler-Puch, has started to nibble away at the market. It is in service as a light prime mover with the UK's rapid reaction forces, and the Desert Gunship version has been tested by the MOD.

four-wheel drive, making them able to tackle the roughest terrain. It was these vehicles which shot to fame in the Scud-buster raids during the 1991 Gulf War.

Weapon load

Typical armament on each DPV consists of a GPMG on the dashboard mount; either a 0.5in Browning machine gun or a Mark 19 automatic grenade launcher on the rear pintle mount; and at least one Milan anti-tank weapon mount. This means that each Land Rover can knock out tanks and other armoured vehicles up to a range of 2000m (6560ft). In addition, LAW 80 short-range anti-armour weapons are carried on every vehicle.

Crew and supplies

Each of the three-man crew is armed with his personal weapon: an M16 rifle fitted with an M203 grenade launcher (see pp.8-11). The

Land Rovers themselves are stuffed full of ammunition, fuel and rations to sustain long-range missions.

As SAS Land Rovers are vulnerable to air attack, each one is equipped with Stinger surface-to-air missiles (SAMs). Altogether, the SAS Land Rover is a fearsome fighting machine.

Crew comfort

Driving and riding in SAS Land Rovers are not particularly pleasant. They are mobile fighting platforms, pure and simple. They are not built for comfort: there are no doors, windscreens or canvas covers. There is thus no protection from the elements, and even the seats are uncomfortable, almost an afterthought. There is also no protection for the crew from enemy gun fire. The engine has armour protection, not the crew. But for mobility and firepower SAS Land Rovers are the best there is.

Below: A variety of weapons can be mounted on Land Rover vehicles, such as this fearsome 0.5in Gatling gun. This flexibility is ideal for units such as the SAS.

GOOD POINTS

✔ SAS Land Rovers have four-wheel drive, making them ideal for off-road use.

✔ They have excellent power-to-weight ratios, as well as good underbelly clearance.

✔ Engines are extremely reliable and they work in extremes of heat and cold.

✔ Their bodies are made of aluminium. They can take a lot of punishment and routine field maintenance can be done during missions themselves.

BAD POINTS

✘ Land Rovers do not have locking axle differentials. This means they can become stuck in some soft ground.

✘ Because of the above point, they require expert drivers to avoid having to be dug out of mud and sand.

✘ They have low-torque engines, which are considered underpowered.

✘ They have a limited range, especially when fully loaded. This means they have to be re-supplied with fuel when operating behind enemy lines.

Left: A 110 Land Rover in traditional garb – armed to the teeth with GPMGs and itching for action.
Inset: SAS 110 Land Rovers in desert camouflage.

HOSTAGE-RESCUE GEAR

SAS ASSAULT TEAM PROTECTION

Above: An SAS soldier, clad in a flameproof black Nomex suit and wearing body armour and SF10 respirator, fires his Browning High Power pistol.

Rescuing hostages is a risky business. SAS soldiers therefore wear clothing that will protect them from bullets, fire, smoke and blast, but will still allow them to go in and get the hostages out alive.

Freeing hostages from the clutches of armed terrorists requires the right equipment. So the SAS has an Operations Research Wing at Stirling Lines, its UK base at Hereford, to test and design hostage-rescue clothing. Its work has resulted in SAS soldiers being kitted out in the best rescue clothing there is.

The requirement

During a hostage-rescue assault SAS soldiers require protection from heat, fire, smoke and blast. They also need protection from any bullets fired by the terrorists.

Protection therefore has to be total. With this in mind SAS soldiers wear special overalls called assault suits. They are made from Nomex, a material that is flameproof. The suit also incorporates a respirator hood and flameproof felt pads in the knees and elbows. The elbow and knee joints are also reinforced by Kevlar (a super-tough plastic compound), which gives protection against sharp objects and allows the wearer to crawl across hot surfaces. For extra protection the men also wear flameproof underwear and gloves. The gloves both protect the hands and ensure a firm grip on weapons and other items of equipment. What about body armour?

Body armour

Over the top of their assault suits SAS soldiers wear assault vests that contain Kevlar plates. So-called 'hard' armour – ceramic composite plates – is worn over the assault vest. The hard armour gives protection against all high-velocity rounds, whereas the assault vests will only stop a standard bullet – a high-velocity bullet travels in excess of 750mps [2460fps].

Though not too heavy, the ceramic plates can weigh up to 4kg (9lb) each, which is tiring to wear on top of everything else. In addition, there is a penalty to pay in terms of freedom of movement: all the gear can restrict manoeuvrability.

Right: A fully equipped SAS hostage-rescue soldier. As well as his assault suit, vest and respirator, he is wearing assault underwear. This is made from carbonised viscose, which is flameproof but also soft and comfortable to wear.

SPECIFICATIONS
Assault vest

Weight	2.5kg (5½lb)
Protection	torso, groin, shoulders, under-arm
Capabilities	will defeat all 5.56mm and 7.62mm rounds

Velcro fasteners

Ceramic contoured plate

Blunt trauma shield

Fragmentation vest

Groin panel

All assault vests also incorporate a so-called 'blunt trauma shield'. Worn underneath the armour, it absorbs and spreads the shock energy of a bullet over a large area.

Helmets

Head protection needs to be taken into account, so SAS soldiers wear helmets that are made from multiple layers of ballistic-resistant composite materials. And they are big enough to be worn over a radio headset.

Because SAS teams will often have to blow in doors and windows with explosives, buildings may catch fire, producing toxic smoke (as in the Iranian Embassy during the SAS hostage-rescue operation in May 1980). SAS soldiers therefore need respirators to breathe properly.

The current SAS respirator is the SF10, which provides full protection. Features include a filter that gives protection against gas and smoke, eye pieces that are resistant to chemicals, and tinted anti-flash lenses.

SPECIFICATIONS
Ballistic helmet

Weight	0.9kg (2lb)
Protection	head
Capabilities	will defeat 5.56mm and 7.62mm rounds

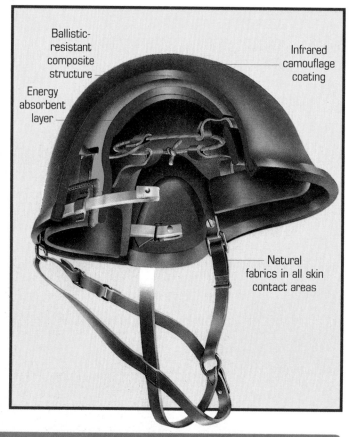

Ballistic-resistant composite structure

Energy absorbent layer

Infrared camouflage coating

Natural fabrics in all skin contact areas

COMPETITORS

Most of the hostage-rescue kit worn by SAS soldiers is produced within the UK. However, because of the close cooperation between the Regiment and its west European and American counterparts, there is a great deal of exchange of ideas regarding hostage-rescue kit. There is therefore very little difference in the type of equipment worn.

West European units, such as the German unit GSG 9 (right), wear body armour and ballistic helmets. The similari-

ty in equipment between the SAS and GSG 9 is obvious: he is armed with a Heckler & Koch MP5 submachine gun, the assault weapon of the SAS, and he wears body armour.

East European units, such as those of the Russian MVD (above) are years behind. One of the above men, for example, is wearing a steel helmet – too heavy and bulky for hostage-rescue.

Left: Modern hostage-rescue equipment is designed to be lightweight to allow team members to move as quickly as possible. When an SAS team bursts into a room full of terrorists and hostages the first few seconds are crucial, so nothing can interfere with the rescuers' freedom of movement.

Left: Communications are essential during a rescue. The respirator therefore incorporates a radio. The microphone itself is mounted in front of the lips.

Air-filled seal

Anti-flash lenses

Microphone cable

One-way diaphragm (outward)

Canister mount (for use with air escape bottle)

Carbon (high levels of protection against incapacitating agents)

Wool

Microphone

SPECIFICATIONS
SF10 respirator

Weight	800g (28oz)
Protection	face
Capabilities	protects wearer from smoke and gases

DEMOLITIONS AND SABOTAGE

Modern explosives mean that SAS soldiers can wreak havoc behind the lines against a host of targets. Bridges, depots, railway lines and command centres are all on the hit list.

In wartime, SAS teams operate deep behind enemy lines. Therefore, the demolition and sabotage of key vulnerable enemy military and industrial targets is one of the most important functions of the Regiment.

What does the SAS hit behind the lines? Sabotage missions will target ports, ships, vehicles, aircraft, bridges, roads, railway lines and depots. In addition, communications centres will be hit, as they are vital to the enemy's command and control network. In this way enemy troop movements will be interrupted. Enemy soldiers will also be tied down with defending sites against sabotage or hunting for saboteurs.

Targets are selected according to their value. Blow a bridge behind the lines during a friendly offensive, for example, and an SAS team can stop enemy reinforcements being sent to where the front has been breached.

Explosives

Once the target has been identified, the next stage is the preparation of equipment. Successful sabotage missions rely on the right type of explosives and their correct placement on the target.

There are two types of explosives: low explosives and high explosives. With low explosives the ignition sequence is set off by a spark or flame. Gunpowder is a good example. Light a match near it and

it will explode. However, when it gets damp it will not work. This is obviously no use to soldiers who often have to operate in wet terrain. Low explosives are therefore rarely used by SAS soldiers, except in home-made devices.

High explosives, as used by the SAS, are much more effective than low explosives. When they are detonated, for example, they produce a shock wave

(blast) that has a great shattering effect. The high explosives used by SAS soldiers include British Army standard-issue PE4 plastic explosive, which was used in the 1991 Gulf War, RDX, PETN, Semtex, M118 demolition charge, Pentolite and Ednatol.

Home-made explosives

Members of the Regiment are also required to have a practical, working knowledge of a third type of explosives. These are home-made 'kitchen sink' explosives. They can be mixed together and used whenever, and wherever, the opportunity arises. Though created from the most mundane domestic ingredients, such as household bleach, garden fertilisers and weed-killers, in the right hands they can be extremely effective.

The Regiment also teaches its personnel to create their own munitions. Even without an 'off the peg' Claymore mine, for example, an SAS team in enemy territory can

Below: The power of modern plastic explosives. In the hands of SAS soldiers charges can be made to cut through steel, shatter concrete and vaporise flesh.

DETONATORS

Electric

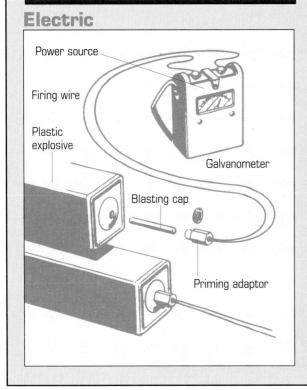

Power source

Firing wire

Plastic explosive

Galvanometer

Blasting cap

Priming adaptor

These diagrams illustrate the two types of detonators used to ignite explosives. With the electric detonator (left), an electrical current flows from a battery to a blasting cap. Inside the cap are two wires, which are connected by means of a bridge wire. When the current is passed through the wires the bridge wire gets hot. The hot bridge wire ignites the charge within the cap, thus detonating the explosive. In the non-electric detonator (right), a hole is made in the explosive (Diagram A). A non-electric blasting cap is inserted into the hole, with a fuse connected to the blasting cap (Diagram B). The blasting cap provides the detonating impulse required to ignite the charge. The fuse consists of gunpowder encased in a fibre wrapping (Diagram C), itself covered with a waterproof material. The fuse is ignited by a flame.

Non-electric

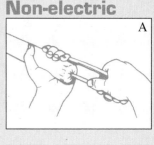

A

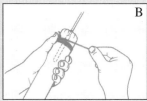

B

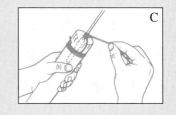

C

still lay an effective ambush. All they need is a plastic container, plastic explosive, detonator and a few nuts and bolts. The result is a home-made Claymore. Connect it to a trip-wire and any enemy patrol stumbling across it will be cut to pieces by shards of hot steel.

Home-made explosives are useful for killing enemy soldiers, but they are of little use against buildings, bridges, tanks or aircraft. They just do not have the destructive force. Larger targets require high explosives, and high explosives require detonators.

Detonators

High explosives cannot be set off without a detonator – an 'initiator'. Take PE4, for example, the type taken behind the lines by the SAS patrol codenamed 'Bravo Two Zero' during the Gulf War. PE4 resembles Plasticine. It can be moulded in the hands. You can jump up and down on it and hit it with a hammer. It can even be set alight. But it will not explode; not without a detonator.

Types of detonator

There are two types of detonator: electric and non-electric. Electric detonators are usually powered by a battery. This sends an electric current into a firing cap, which in turn explodes, detonating the explosive. A non-electric detonator can serve as a back-up device should the main detonator be disabled. This simple set-up consists of a blasting cap connect-

ed to a length of fuse cord which is made from black powder – gunpowder – wrapped in fibre. This has the benefit of simplicity, in that there are no electrics to go wrong. All that needs to happen is for the fuse cord to be set alight.

Above: It looks harmless. However, this mine is packed with explosive. Step on it and it will take your leg off.

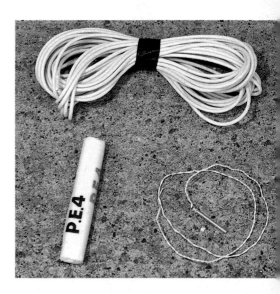

Above: What every SAS soldier has tucked in his bergen: PE4 plastic explosive (left), the kind used by the SAS during the 1991 Gulf War; an electric detonator (right); and a length of detonating cord (top).

BRIDGE DEMOLITION

When destroying bridges, SAS teams will place charges in such a way that they will cause the bridge to become unstable. In this way the weight of the bridge itself can be used to bring it crashing down. Diagram A shows how six charges can demolish a concrete cantilever bridge with sus-

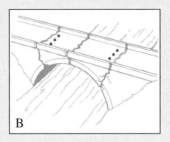

B

pended span. When the charges go off, the cantilever arms adjacent to the suspended arch are cut. In this way the suspended span collapses. Diagram B shows how a filled spandrel bridge is destroyed. Here the charges are much more 'bunched' to blow the whole bridge, rather than cutting sections of it. When tackling continuous span truss bridges (Diagram C), SAS teams will

plant charges as shown. The bridge will become unstable when the explosives are detonated, causing it to collapse. A girder arch bridge (Diagram D) can be weakened in a similar fashion. Cutting the steel supports will cause the bridge to become dangerously unstable. Even if it does not collapse, it will not support heavy loads. Suspension bridges (Diagram E) are relatively easy to demolish.

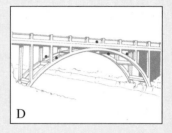

D

The charges are placed on the towers slightly above the roadway, and on the cables near the top of the towers. When they go off, the bridge collapses.

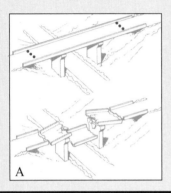

A

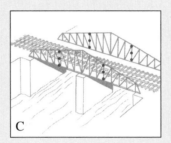

C

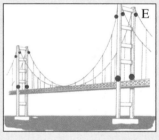

E

An SAS team will not always want to set off the explosives as soon as they are set. Therefore, timers are always carried on missions.

Timers

SAS timers used to be of a crude crush delay variety, which were essentially copper tubes filled with acid. Along the tube ran a lead wire. When the tube was crushed, the acid would eat through the lead, which would then release a spring. This in turn would set off a flash compound, which would go off into the detonator, igniting the explosive. The thickness of the lead wire governed the timing of the fuse – anything from 10 seconds to five hours.

The disadvantage with this timer was its inaccuracy and tendency to be affected by the weather. As one SAS veteran described the dangers of setting the 10-second fuse: 'You had to be a bit of a genius with the weather to work out what the temperature was.'

Electronics have now revolutionised timers, which can be set for any time from nine seconds to 99 years. To

increase their capabilities and destructive potential, they can also lie dormant, restarting themselves at various times in order to recharge. At any given time, they can be activated by a radio signal, releasing a charge of perhaps no more than 0.3 of a milli-amp, setting off the explosive device.

State-of-the-art timers

The advantage of devices made with this kind of transponder-type timer is that, once placed and hidden, they can lay in wait for years until detonated. Such bombs have been used by the IRA in Northern Ireland. To defend against them and to initiate a premature detonation, British Army patrols have used electronic counter-measures, sending out ahead of them radio signals at various frequencies. The introduction of sophisticated 28-day timers into domestic electrical equipment, such as video recorders, has made

Right: Setting explosive charges on a bridge. Such sabotage can seriously affect enemy troop and material movements. As such, it is part of SAS demolitions training.

access to this kind of advanced technology – and its use in bomb-making – commonplace today.

Having the right tools for the job is one part of successful sabotage. The other is the correct placement of the charges themselves.

Laying charges

In carrying out an act of sabotage, careful planning and a thorough reconnaissance of the target is vital. It is essential that the target is studied and its potential weaknesses identified. The object of any attack is to create the maximum amount of damage with the minimum amount of explosive. This can only be achieved with correct placement of charges.

To achieve maximum effect, a charge of plastic explosive is usually placed in what is known as a '2:1 shape'. This means that on the target the charge is twice as high as it is wide. In this way the shock waves go down into the target. It is the same with the detonator. If it is placed at the end of a flat charge, then a

lot of the force of the subsequent explosion will be lost sideways. The most efficient way is to place the detonator on top of the charge so that the shock waves go down into the target, creating the maximum destructive effect.

The need to make the very best use of available explosives is a cornerstone of SAS demolitions training. Since everything of use to the operation must be carried, and the object of a mission of sabotage is to infiltrate, destroy and escape in the fastest possible time, then every kilogram of explosive must be used to maximum effect.

Booby traps

Even abandoned equipment can be put to good use with a small amount of explosive. The booby-trapped kit can be left behind to be found by the enemy. Anyone who touches it will have his hand blown off at least – a good way to slow down a pursuing enemy unit.

The efficient use of explosives has increased a great deal since the 1960s.

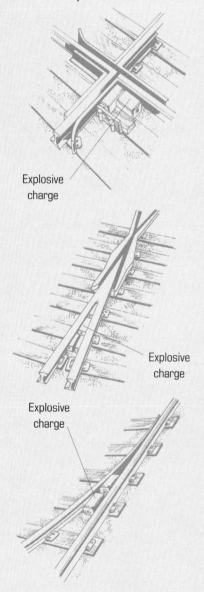

SAS teams targeting railway lines will, where possible, try to place explosives where they will cause the maximum effect. This means placing them on points and intersections (as shown below). Laying charges on stretches of straight track can be counter-productive, as these sections can be replaced relatively easily. Wrecked points and intersections mean that two lines at least will be temporarily out of action, thus increasing the disruption to the enemy's communications system.

Explosive charge

Explosive charge

Explosive charge

Before then common practice was to use solid charges on objects and destroy them by sheer explosive force. For example, a steel bar 178mm (7in) in diameter, using this method, would need a bulky, solid charge of 6.8kg (15lb) to cut it. Though fail-safe, this was inefficient and a waste of explosive.

Less is more

The development of more sophisticated demolition methods, pioneered in the United States in the 1960s, taught that less explosive could be made to do the

DESTRUCTION OF AIRCRAFT

Modern military aircraft are fearsome fighting machines in the air. But on the ground they are very vulnerable to attack, especially from elite units. They are basically shells stuffed full of sophisticated, and fragile, avionics and machinery. Sabotaging them is therefore very easy. SAS teams will place explosives where indicated on the diagram below: on the nose cones (which contain radar and avionics), undercarriage, air intakes and exhausts. Only a small charge is required to ground the most sophisticated flying machine. Even small-arms fire, as used by the SAS against Argentinian aircraft on Pebble Island in the Falklands, is sufficient to render an aircraft useless.

same job. The basis of this new demolition method was the shaped charge. Instead of a solid mass of explosive on the steel bar, the structure and the shape of the bar would be taken into consideration and exploited. Thus, a diamond-shaped charge of only 1.36kg (3lb) had the same explosive effect as a solid mass of explosive five times larger. It was

Right: A wrecked Argentinian Pucara aircraft on the Pebble Island airstrip after the SAS's raid during the Falklands War. Explosive charges have blown off the undercarriage and nose cone.

a system of demolition that meant the same effect could be achieved with less explosive. For units such as the SAS it was a godsend. For one thing it meant that foot patrols could carry out more sabotage missions with the same amount of explosives. The

Regiment embraced it readily, sending personnel over to the United States to learn the method at first hand.

In choosing the targets for sabotage or demolition, an SAS soldier will always take the practical approach. He will always go for the key points on any target. In attacking the industry of an enemy state, for example, an SAS team would target its electricity supply by

EYEWITNESS

The Raid on Berka Airfield
March 1942

'We hit the perimeter at about midnight and saw German sentries. As usual, we waited until they had walked by our position and then shot across the road into the trees on the other side. Then we split into two groups. We went for the bombers lying under the cover of the trees. We just walked down the line [of aircraft] lobbing Lewes bombs on to their wings. When the job was finished, Paddy [Mayne] and I sped out of the place. We halted later for a break and the bombers started to go up – it must have been about two hours as we were using time pencils of that duration.'

Sergeant-Major Bob Bennett, L Detachment

destroying power lines and the turbines in power stations. As a method of disrupting the running of any industrial organisation, the targeting of computers and records is also an option, as is the identification and killing of key maintenance personnel.

With their great adaptability, explosives are of enormous use not just in industrial sabotage but also in the field. SAS personnel are trained to blow up roads, bridges and railways and to use explosives to clear jungle and forests to create airstrips. They are also trained to use explosives offensively, setting them in ambushes to trap and kill an enemy.

The Claymore mine
The Claymore mine is a favourite piece of equipment in the offensive role. The Claymore comprises a concave plate, on which is layered plastic explosive and 350 metal balls. Once detonated, by trip wire or electric contact, the balls are blown out, devastating an area up to a range of 100m (328ft).

These sophisticated methods of demolition are taught to members of the Regiment on the Advanced Demolition Course. This is a supplement to the Basic Course which, over an intensive 10-week period, teaches SAS personnel the basic methods and safety procedures related to explosives and incendiary sabotage. Though there is a large written test at the end of the course, the instruction is mostly practical.

In the past disused factories and power stations throughout Britain have been used to simulate targets. In this way members of the Regiment were given practical experience of planning and executing attacks. To give their training a further degree of reality, a number of working power stations have also been used. These simulated attacks – using dummy explosives, of course – have also

helped in planning the defence of these establishments against attack. The Regiment has also gone abroad on these exercises, simulating attacks on industrial facilities in northern Europe. This training also included potential operations against nuclear facilities. During the stand-off of the Cold War, it was part of the West's operational plan to slow down the Warsaw Pact's advance by destroying nuclear power stations. This would create areas of lethal radioactivity.

The multi-skilled SAS soldier
An SAS soldier, fully trained in the methods of demolitions and sabotage, is able to call upon an enormous variety of skills. For the successful sabotage of key enemy sites and structures an SAS man has to be many things. He has to be a structural engineer, able to locate targets. He has to be a mathematician, able to calculate the areas and weights of targets in relation to the force of the explosive employed. He has to be an electrician, capable of rigging circuits and working out the electrical resistance. He must also have nerves of steel, both to handle highly dangerous substances and to plant them on the target. In all, combined with his combat skills, the ability to destroy and disable targets with explosives is a very powerful weapon in the hands of an SAS soldier.

TANK KILLING

Tanks are easy to disable with explosives. However, as they have armour to defeat anti-tank rounds, charges must be sited precisely to achieve the desired effect. As indicated on the diagrams, charges should be placed on the tracks and underneath the hull (right), and under turret rings and on top of the engines (below). Only a charge underneath a tank is likely to kill the crew.

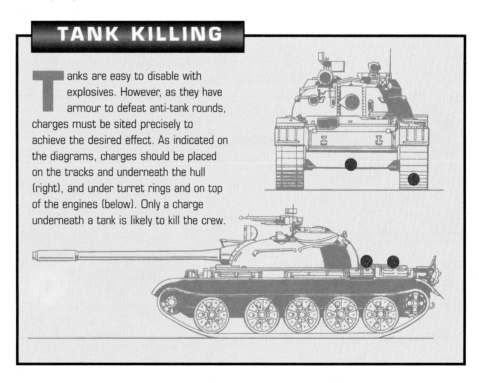

AMBUSH OPERATIONS

SAS ambushes are quick and lethal. The boys who wear the Winged Dagger badge are experts when it comes to turning enemy infantry into corpses and hostile tanks and armoured vehicles into burning piles of scrap metal.

One of the most effective tactics the SAS uses against an enemy is the ambush. It is a method of taking offensive action which takes both skill and cunning to execute, but which can reap enormous benefits and inflict terrible damage.

The SAS sees the ambush as fulfilling a number of vital functions. Its most obvious use is that it can take an enemy force, particularly an infantry unit, unawares and destroy it. In addition, an ambush can also be used defensively. Just the threat of an ambush can prevent an enemy gaining access to a secure base

area, and provide protection for that base. An ambush can also be used to take enemy prisoners and gather valuable intelligence, and at the same time destroy the enemy's morale.

Siting an ambush

The success of an ambush relies almost entirely on surprise. Therefore, the correct placing and timing of an ambush is one of the SAS's most practised fighting skills. To begin with, an ambush party must always be where it is least expected. Enemy soldiers on patrol, or on the move, will be on maximum alert. They

Above: Russian troops caught in a Mujahadeen ambush in the Afghan War. A well-laid ambush, such as this one and those sprung by the SAS, can annihilate an enemy unit in seconds.

will be watching any areas that look as if they might be used for an ambush. Paths through gorges or tracks next to rivers are ideal ambush places, because they are areas where movement and escape is limited. It is therefore the job of the SAS ambush commander to out-think the enemy, and to place his men where the enemy least expect an attack, and where he will be at a clear advantage.

Hitting an enemy when he is at his most tired is one way to catch him off guard. An enemy force at the end of a long day's march, or near the end of a steep climb, will not be as fresh and alert as one that has just started marching.

The whole object of choosing the ground for an ambush – known as 'the killing ground' – is to find a place where the enemy can be confined and where exit points can be blocked or booby-trapped. A place with no escape.

Choosing the place is one thing, but having the right tools for the job is just as important. The weapons the SAS uses in an ambush will depend on the type of terrain. In close country, such as jungle, submachine guns or assault rifles are used. These will normally be the 5.56mm M16 rifle and 9mm Heckler & Koch MP5 submachine gun.

Air filled with lead

The rate of fire of these weapons is very high – the MP5, for example, fires at an incredible rate of 15 rounds per second. Though their effective range is comparatively short, this does not matter since ambushes in such dense terrain are usually made at very close quarters – when the

SAS team can see the whites of the enemy's eyes. These lighter weapons also have the advantage of being easy to conceal and camouflage.

Heavier machine guns such as the GPMG tend not to be used in close country, because their bipods are difficult to hide. Also, the sheer size of the weapon would disturb the undergrowth and give away the position of the ambush team. Bigger machine guns also need wider arcs of fire, which again require the clearing of a great deal of undergrowth. This could easily be spotted by the enemy, destroying the vitally important element of surprise.

The kiss of the Claymore

Explosives can be extremely efficient weapons in an ambush. The Claymore mine, which can explode its contents of 300 metal balls across a range of 100m (328ft), is an ideal weapon for trapping an enemy. It is small, light, easily concealed and devastatingly lethal. Each ball will go through flesh like a hot knife through butter.

Grenades are also extremely useful. Set up in undergrowth on their own or in groups, they can, like Claymores, be

LINEAR AMBUSH

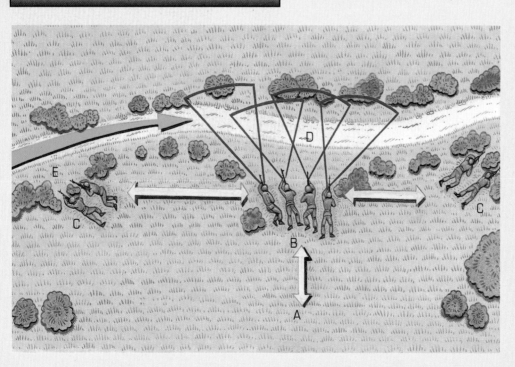

This diagram illustrates the classic SAS linear ambush. The commander takes his team to the laying-up position (A). All the bergens and heavy equipment are left here. Then the team advances to the ambush point (B). A covering group is assigned to each flank (C). The killing ground, where the enemy soldiers will be shot dead, is covered by overlapping fields of fire (D). The ambush is sprung once the main enemy force (E) is in the killing ground. After the ambush enemy dead will be searched for intelligence purposes. Then the SAS team retreats to the laying-up point.

Above: During the bush war against nationalist guerrillas in the 1970s, a Rhodesian SAS patrol reacts after being ambushed. The SAS soldiers instinctively charge the enemy ambush team.

These six photographs show a simulated SAS ambush using non-SAS personnel. They show the ideal type of terrain for ambush operations, as well as the importance of camouflage skills for the ambush to work. Note how difficult it is to spot those soldiers in photograph D!

A The ambush party moves out from the laying-up point towards the ambush site, taking care to disturb as little foliage as possible.

B At the site the ambush is prepared. The commander ensures that his men are positioned in such a way that their fields of fire overlap. Note the undisturbed foliage to the front.

C The enemy patrol moves cautiously forward. Each man scans the area for any telltale signs of the enemy, ready to fire his weapon instantly.

D Successful ambushes demand excellent camouflage and concealment skills. One tiny slip and the mission will be compromised.

E Once the ambush has been set there remains nothing to do but wait for the enemy. There is absolute quiet.

F The ambush is sprung. The enemy patrol is caught in a hail of fire. Some of them try to return fire and others attempt to flee, but to no avail. Within seconds they are all dead.

rigged to trip wires to explode in the path of an unsuspecting enemy. These explosive ambushes have the advantage that they can lay in position for weeks, even months. And trip wires mean that enemy soldiers will be cut to pieces whatever direction they come from.

Manpower requirements

These explosive ambushes can be set up by a small number of men. Using a large number of Claymores, wired together to be electrically detonated from a single command position, for example, it would be possible for a large ambush to be sprung by just one man. The SAS , however, keeps the minimum number of men in an ambush to four. This gives the team all-round cover and mutual support if it is counterattacked. Usually the number of men in an ambush is determined by the size of the enemy unit they are attacking. If the enemy unit is in

COUNTER-AMBUSH TACTICS

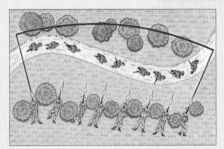 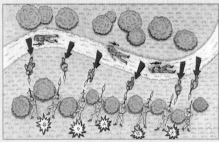 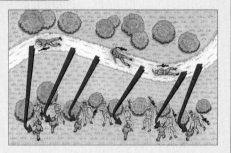

An enemy unit lies in wait, ready to ambush a passing SAS patrol. The SAS patrol marches down the path in single file. The enemy waits until the whole patrol is in the killing field before opening fire. All the members of the enemy unit have overlapping fields of fire. Several SAS soldiers are killed instantaneously. The SAS patrol then charges the enemy ambush team.

Several SAS soldiers are killed instantaneously, but the rest react at once. They do not make a dash for the trees on the other side of the path – they may be booby-trapped. Instead, they begin firing and throwing grenades at the ambushers. It takes guts to charge at a concealed enemy who is firing at you, but only by getting in among the foe does an ambushed SAS unit stand a chance.

The enemy soldiers, shocked and disorientated, abandon their positions and attempt to flee. However, the SAS soldiers are too quick and cut them down before they can retreat. The SAS men then leave at speed. The quick reaction times of the SAS soldiers and their ability to bring heavy firepower to bear on a target has saved their unit from being wiped out.

strength, then so is the SAS lying in wait to destroy it.

Reconnaissance

In planning an ambush, good reconnaissance is essential. The ambush team will study aerial photographs, maps and local intelligence to find out which route the enemy is taking and to choose the right spot for the attack. Ambushes are usually made on lines of enemy communication, such as roads and paths, where the ambush team are assured of a target.

The chosen area will then be carefully checked out. The team commander will be looking for a position of good cover which allows his men a clear shot at the enemy. However, he will still want enough cover to protect his own men should the enemy get a chance to fire back. Once he is sure he has the right spot, the commander will then lead his men to a laying-up point behind his line of fire. In some cases this can be up to 1000m (3300ft) to the rear. The laying-up position will be the team's fall-back and rendezvous (RV) point after the attack. It is also the place where the bergens and other heavy kit is stored.

The linear ambush

The commander will then lead his men forward and set them up in their ambush positions. The favoured SAS tactic is the linear ambush. The men are set up in front of the killing ground and organised so that they have overlapping fields of fire. Two sets of men are then sent out to cover each flank and to give advance warning of the enemy's approach.

When taking up their positions, the SAS team will make sure that the undergrowth surrounding them, particularly that directly in front of their guns, is left completely undisturbed. The approaching enemy must see nothing suspicious.

The ambush team now lie and wait. The wait could be for hours, it could even be for days. The SAS men will wait for as long as it takes for the enemy to arrive. Tension among team members is high, almost unbearable.

Springing an ambush

If the enemy are sensible, then they will have an advance party scouting ahead of the main group. The SAS soldiers let them through unharmed. The object of the ambush is to take out the main party. When it finally arrives in front of the barrels of the ambush team, then all hell breaks loose. The killing ground quickly becomes littered with dead. The action is over in seconds.

The SAS teaches that a successful ambush is one where the enemy are so caught by surprise that they are all killed before they have time to react. Because of the superior weapons skills of SAS soldiers this is usually the case – no one gets out alive.

Overwhelming firepower

Why are most enemy personnel killed in SAS ambushes? The answer is heavy firepower. In the space of a few seconds the SAS team will fire hundreds of rounds of ammunition. In Northern Ireland on 8 May 1987, for example, just over 30 SAS soldiers ambushed an IRA team in the village of Loughall. In the space of a few seconds the SAS fired over 1200 rounds, killing all eight of the IRA terrorists in a spectacular action. But what happens when SAS soldiers themselves are caught in ambushes?

Counter-ambush tactics

If an SAS team is caught in an ambush there is a chance they will all be killed. However, if enough of them survive the first seconds under fire, the Regiment's standard counter-ambush tactic is for the ambushed soldiers to pour fire towards the ambushers. Hopefully this will make them take cover and cease firing. Then the SAS soldiers will rush their position. It sounds a dangerous manoeuvre, even a reckless one, but it is the best response in

EYEWITNESS

Northern France
June 1944

'We had about 10 minutes before the action would commence. From my position I observed the two leading motorcyclists come up the slope and disappear around the bend to be clobbered by Ian Welstead. At the same moment the first three-tonner crammed with soldiers drew level... and over came the plastic bombs. One hit the bonnet and the other the rear of the vehicle. Pandemonium among the occupants. Many were killed by fire from the *Maquis* as they fled across the road towards open fields. Our Brens opened up with devastating effect and many of the [enemy troops] retreated back to the ditch, which was in Reg's sights. It was a massacre.'

Lieutenant-Colonel Johnny Cooper
1st SAS Regiment

a very precarious situation. To run away from an ambush may mean running straight into enemy booby traps, or even another ambush.

After a successful attack, an SAS ambush team will want to get out fast. If they have time they will check the enemy dead for any useful intelligence. If they haven't, then they will make an exit along their line of withdrawal, taking any of their wounded with them.

The whole object of an SAS ambush is to arrive unseen, hit very hard, and then disappear before the enemy has a chance to discover what has happened.

An ambush is a superbly lethal tactic at the best of times, but as used by the soldiers of the SAS it can bring war to an enemy in places he would never expect. This can have a very demoralising effect on an enemy – nowhere is safe from the Special Air Service.

Above: Rhodesian SAS soldiers return fire during a contact with terrorist guerrillas in the Rhodesian bush in 1975. Counter-ambush tactics require excellent weapon skills.

Left: After a successful ambush, if there is time, the enemy are searched for intelligence-gathering purposes.

FREEFALL PARACHUTING

Leaving an aircraft at high altitudes to land undetected in enemy territory is what SAS freefall parachuting is all about. But it takes a lot of guts to carry out an operational freefall, plus specialised knowledge to avoid all the hazards involved.

No matter what their other individual fighting skills might be, all the members of the SAS are qualified parachutists, trained to jump out of an aircraft using a static line: a line connected to the aircraft which pulls open the parachute as the man falls. This is the standard method of military parachuting and allows large numbers of troops to be dropped from an aircraft from heights as low as 120m (400ft).

SAS combat freefallers

There is a troop within each SAS Sabre Squadron, though, which is also trained in the dangerous and more specialised form of parachuting known as combat freefall. In this technique, fully-armed and equipped soldiers, usually wearing oxygen equipment, jump from aircraft at heights of up to 12,000m (40,000ft) and above, using their own bodies to literally fly towards the landing zone (LZ), before opening their 'chutes and drifting onto the target area.

The Regiment uses two main methods of freefall jumping: High Altitude, Low Opening (HALO), and High Altitude, High Opening (HAHO). Both these freefall techniques are dangerous, and it is accepted by the Regiment that if they are used operationally then there will be

Left: Members of The Parachute Regiment's Pathfinder Platoon carry out a High Altitude, Low Opening (HALO) jump.
Below: The tense moments before a jump.

casualties. However, as a final option freefall is the perfect way of inserting a team into territory where the enemy has cut off every other means of approach. It also gives SAS soldiers a way of getting into a country without the aircraft carrying them having to fly into hostile air space, where it could be spotted and shot down. Using HAHO, for example, a trooper can be dropped outside a country's border and drift up to 32km

(20 miles) before landing. If the target country does not possess sophisticated radars, then there is a good chance that the trooper can reach his LZ undetected.

SAS parachutes

The basic type of parachute used in SAS freefall operations is known as the TAP, the Tactical Assault Parachute. It has a square canopy divided up into a series of cells which enables the jumper to control the direction and speed of his descent with great accuracy.

Below: An RAF Hercules transport aircraft flies low over the Scottish west coast during a special forces training exercise. SAS Freefall Troops use Hercules to carry out drops.

When fully kitted-up for action, the SAS freefall specialist looks as weighed down and cumbersome as it is possible for a man to be. He is carrying his belt equipment on his waist, the parachute on his back and his assault rifle secured, usually, behind his shoulder on the left-hand side. He will also be carrying his bergen beneath the parachute, secured by harnesses around his legs to clips on his front. If he is the team signaller, then he will also be carrying a radio. In most drops the freefaller will also be carrying a small bottle of oxygen.

Oxygen is used in freefall depending on the height of the jump and the length of time the parachutist is going to spend in the air. As a rule, oxygen is used when jumping from an altitude of over 3600m (12,000ft), though it has been used when dropping from 1500m (5000ft).

Exiting the aircraft

Operationally, freefallers go on to oxygen 30 minutes before they jump. The pilot de-pressurises the aircraft and the team plug into the aircraft's oxygen supply. They will only plug into their own

oxygen five minutes before jump time. By this time the pilot will have turned into the wind and be on his final approach to the dropping point, warning the drop team by turning the red light in the aircraft to green.

In any freefall operation, this is one of the most critical times. If the freefaller does not exit the aircraft at exactly the right time and place he could be carried way off target, perhaps with disastrous results. The problem lies in the fact that, unlike static-line jumping, where he is jumping so low that he is almost on top

4

This sequence of photographs shows the procedure for a special forces High Altitude, Low Open (HALO) freefall parachute descent. The drop is being made from an altitude of 7500m (25,000ft) from an RAF Hercules long-range transport aircraft over Herefordshire.

1 The team shuffles forward towards the aircraft's rear ramp. They are all breathing their own oxygen now, having been previously plugged into the aircraft's oxygen supply.

2 The team leaves the aircraft. Seconds before each man has been weighed down with main 'chute, reserve, bergen, belt kit and personal weapon. But now they feel light as feathers as they begin their descent.

3 As they fall, the four-man patrol begins to group. Note the bergens.

4 The four-man patrol groups as the Hercules disappears into the distance.

of the LZ, the freefaller is a long way from his LZ and must drift on to it. This skill the SAS man must learn to perfect.

The descent

His difficulties begin the moment he leaves the aircraft. As he jumps, he will be travelling at the aircraft's speed – probably about 160kmph (100mph). This means that he will be thrown forward of the aircraft in the first moments of his descent. As he slows down to freefall, though, the oncoming wind will pick him up and carry him back, So when he opens his parachute canopy, he will be a long way behind the point at which

After the freefall descent the team will deploy their 'chutes and unclip their bergens before they land.

1 At a height of 900m (3000ft) the GQ360 parachutes leave their packs.

2 The canopy inflates, rapidly slowing the rate of descent.

3 The team lands together so the men can assemble quickly at the landing zone.

4 Each man unclips his bergen prior to landing.

he actually jumped. He now has to identify the LZ on the ground, judge the strength of the wind and the distance to target to guide his parachute in. When choosing the moment to open the canopy, the freefaller must always make the most practical decision. If, for example, he is going over a bad landing area and heading for better ground, then he will delay deploying his canopy to ensure a good landing.

Pre-landing drills

Whatever the conditions on the ground, and no matter from what height the freefaller jumps, as a matter of operational security his canopy must be fully deployed at 900m (3000ft). This is because if it happens any lower, the sound of the canopy opening can be heard clearly from the ground, which could compromise a secret SAS mission.

Another key point is the moment at which the bergen pack is released. Once the canopy is fully deployed, the parachutist unclips his bergen, which then drops to hang suspended from a strap 4.5m (15ft) below him. If it is dropped too early the bergen can get entangled in the rigging of other men's parachutes, or even drag the parachutist himself onto power lines or other overhead cables.

To make sure that his canopy opens at the right altitude, each SAS freefaller carries an automatic parachute-opening device, which operates when the air pressure – which is governed by altitude – reaches a certain point. It is also a fail-safe device which operates even if the parachutist is unable to open his own 'chute in an emergency.

Emergency procedures

The SAS freefaller must also be prepared if something goes wrong: if his canopy doesn't deploy correctly, or if it becomes entangled on itself and collapses. In such emergencies his main canopy can be jet-

Above: At the landing zone (LZ) the men deploy flares and markers to guide in follow-on teams. On active missions such measures would be forbidden for security reasons.

tisoned by releasing a securing clip on either shoulder. As the man falls free, and the main canopy flies off, a static line goes with it and pulls open the smaller, reserve, 'chute, which is held piggy-back fashion above it.

Another hazard is colliding with other team members, particularly if the jump is being done at night. For this reason each SAS soldier carries a fluorescent silum stick on the back of his pack.

SNIPING

The SAS sniper is a soldier who works alone, a man who has to have great courage and patience to lie close to the enemy and wait for his target. He must also have ice-cool nerves to be able to kill without compassion.

Above: Sniping is an art, and SAS snipers are the masters at it. As well as good camouflage skills, snipers must have good eyesight, patience, courage and the all-important 'will to kill'. SAS snipers have them all in abundance.

The SAS uses sniping for a number of important jobs. The first – and most 'traditional' – is the killing of key enemy targets such as officers and HQ staff, and the lowering of the enemy's morale. The threat of hidden snipers can also act like the risk of booby traps and stop an enemy trying to gain access to an area, while the ability of the sniper to lie unseen within rifle range of the enemy also makes him the ideal man to collect information and intelligence. No matter what his mission, though, the sniper is always fully briefed before he is deployed. He must know what he is targeting before he goes into action.

Sniper rifles

The type of mission he is on will also dictate the type of rifle he will use. The British Army usually uses just one sniper rifle – the 7.62mm Accuracy International L96A1. The SAS sniper, though, has a choice of three versions of the L96A1, each one specially adapted for a particular kind of target. These are his 'Hard Kill' and 'Soft Kill' weapons, and a special rifle with a fitted silencer.

The 'Hard Kill' rifle is designed for outdoor work and is designed to hit a head target at 600m (1968ft – nearly a third of a mile). The 'Soft Kill' weapon is designed for targets inside an enclosed space, such as a building under siege. In this kind of operation, the sniper doesn't want to fire a bullet so powerful that it could go right through the gunman into an innocent hostage. The 'Soft Kill' weapon therefore fires a slower, heavier round with a smaller calibre whose range is only 300m (984ft). Once again the target would be the head. Snipers don't go for body shots. The chance of hitting body armour or failing to kill the target with one round is a risk SAS snipers don't take.

The rifles are all bolt-action, with heavy, 'free-floating' barrels: the barrels are not secured to the rifle's stock, which could lead to inaccuracy. Both 'Hard Kill' and 'Soft Kill' weapons have interchangeable day and night sights.

Sniper ammunition

For hitting targets over long ranges, using the right ammunition is also vital. SAS snipers use what is known as 'Green Spot' ammunition, which has been specially manufactured to a very high degree of accuracy. The ammunition comes in batches, all of which have been made to exactly the same specifications. This means that when a sniper

Below: A sniper with the current British Army sniper rifle – the 7.62mm Accuracy International PM. This gun, which has a 10-round magazine, is also used by SAS snipers to pick off targets up to 1000m (3280ft) away.

Right: When in his hide, an SAS sniper will only allow the end of his barrel to protrude. The rest of the weapon will be hidden and covered in hessian.

Far right: A sniper tailors his camouflage to the environment he is working in. The idea is to completely break up his outline and the outline of his weapon. But it is not just a case of lying in a hole in the ground and covering up with bits of foliage. SAS snipers must have a thorough knowledge of the principles of concealment, which revolve around proper siting, construction of hides and discipline.

Far right, inset: A sniper in a so-called Gillie suit – an item of clothing of dyed hessian strips.

zeros in his bolt-action rifle with one shot, he knows that the rest of the rounds in the batch will perform in exactly the same way.

Finding the right location

The accuracy of his rifles will be totally wasted, though, if the sniper cannot get into position within range of the enemy. This is where his fieldcraft and skills of camouflage and concealment come into play. In the field the SAS sniper wears a Gillie suit of dyed hessian strips, which breaks up his shape and profile. He also blackens his face and removes from his pockets everything which might move and make a noise. His weapon, except for the breech and the end of the barrel (known as 'the lead'), is also covered in hessian.

The SAS sniper will move into position at night, preferably in bad weather. He will leave his bergen at a laying-up point (LUP) at a distance behind his final shooting position – known as his 'hide'. Moving up to this point, which will be 600-1000m (1968-3282ft) from the enemy, he will zero-in his rifle and then wait for his target to appear.

His best method of concealment in the hide will be to stay motionless behind undisturbed undergrowth, with only the lead of his rifle barrel showing through. Thankfully he will not need to keep his rifle in his shoulder all the time. Most sniper rifles are fitted with both a bipod on the stock and an adjustable spigot in the butt, so he will only need to hold it long enough to get it adjusted to the right position. As for the length of time he will have to wait, one SAS veteran, when asked the question, replied: 'How long? For a lifetime if he has to.'

The SAS sniper has his LUP to go back to for food and sleep, but until his target arrives in his sights, he will spend every possible moment in his hide with only his rifle and a water bottle.

The art of killing at long range really comes into play when the target eventually appears. The sniper will estimate the distance – perhaps by using a laser designator – and register it on his scope, which will give him his elevation. He will then make his final sight adjust-

The Radfan, Aden
April 1964

'I was laying up in an OP overlooking a deep wadi, up in the mountains of the Radfan near the Yemeni border. It was hell on earth in those temperatures. The sunset brought some relief and let me get to a well nearby to draw water. On the way down I spotted two guerrillas who obviously had the same idea. I got into position behind loose rocks and brought them into my sights. They were about 365m (1200ft) away and night was falling fast. The lead man went down with a round to the head, and his mate didn't even have time to raise his weapon before I'd dropped him too.'

Name withheld for security reasons

ments to compensate for any wind or rain, and when he is sure of his aim, a mere touch of his fingertip on the trigger will fire the round. There is no safety catch to delay his shot – SAS sniper rifles don't have them. Once the bullet is in the breech it is either used or unloaded. Most of the time it is used.

The sniper kill

If his markmanship is as good as it should be, the SAS sniper will see his target go down – the head blown apart by a high-velocity round. His next task will be to avoid getting caught. The enemy will have his range – the time between the report of the rifle and the 'thump' of the bullet on target will give

Above: SAS snipers are trained to operate in all terrain types. It takes a special kind of marksman to hit a human head at a range of 1000m (3280ft).

them that – but they will not know from which direction the bullet came. Immediately after he has fired, therefore, the sniper must remain absolutely still. Any movement will give the enemy a target. He will thus have to wait until things have quietened down before he leaves the hide, goes back to his bergen and follows his escape route away from the scene. As with most things associated with the SAS, sniping is fairly simple, but requires nerves of steel and the patience of a saint.

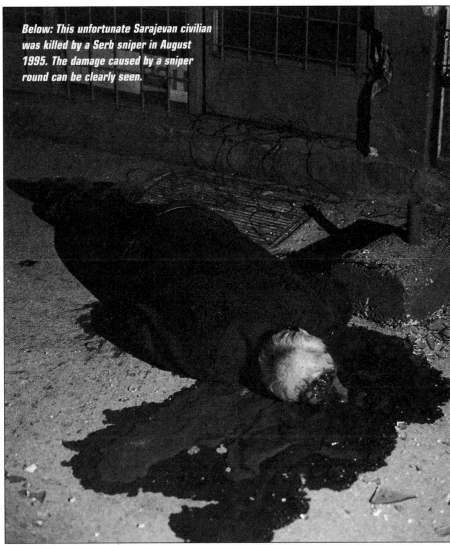

Below: This unfortunate Sarajevan civilian was killed by a Serb sniper in August 1995. The damage caused by a sniper round can be clearly seen.

niping is an art which requires meticulous preparation to perfect. The SAS sniper is both feared and loathed by the enemy, and he knows that if he is captured he is unlikely to live – he therefore leaves nothing to chance.

1 Before he moves forward to his hide, the sniper will camouflage himself to blend into his surroundings.

2 In addition to the sights fitted to his rifle, the sniper will often have other scopes to observe his target area closely before he takes his shot.

3 When it comes to taking the shot a sniper must remain calm – he will only get one chance.

HOSTAGE-RESCUE: BUILDINGS

Storming buildings to free hostages from armed terrorists is a specialist job. SAS soldiers must be able to get in quickly and sweep through a building to get to the hostages before they are killed. Such work requires split-second timing.

ostage-rescue from buildings is a vital part of the SAS's anti-terrorist operations. As the Regiment proved at the siege of the Iranian Embassy in London in May 1980, for example, when it comes to breaking armed sieges and rescuing hostages, it is among the world's finest.

But the armed assault is just the final stage in the sequence of SAS operations in an armed siege. Initially the whole focus of activity is in building up detailed intelligence about the building, the hostages, and of course 'the bad guys'.

The first step is to seal off the building and the surrounding area. This isolates the hostage-takers and provides room for the Regiment to position its own men out of the glare of publicity. Remember, the terrorists will probably have access to

Left: An SAS team storms a building during a training exercise. Only countless hours spent perfecting clearing buildings will guarantee success when it's for real.
Below: Doing it for real – the SAS storms the Iranian Embassy in May 1980. The entire operation took only 17 minutes.

radio and television, so secrecy is of the utmost importance.

The first SAS units in position will be the snipers. Their job will be to recce the building, keep watch on any movement inside, and, if an assault goes in, act as a possible diversion by taking out any of the terrorists stupid enough to show themselves. The snipers will be linked to the SAS commander on the ground by means of portable radios.

Talking surrender

Getting the terrorists involved in negotiations is the next move. This will be undertaken by trained police personnel, and serves two main functions. The first, of course, is to persuade the terrorists to give up. Failing that, though, the negotiations strengthen the hand of the military option by helping to identify the gunmen, and perhaps even help to locate the hostages in the building.

Talking to the terrorists may also secure the release of some of the hostages, especially if any are pregnant

Above: If the doors are barred for any reason, the windows provide another way of getting into a building during a hostage-rescue. Below: When the door is kicked or blown in the assault team throws in stun grenades.

Above: Submachine guns and pistols are the primary weapons when an SAS team clears a building. This man is armed with a Browning High Power pistol, which was used during the storming of the Iranian Embassy in May 1980.

women, old or injured in any way, and this is where the best intelligence will come from. If it is going to have to attack the building, the SAS will want as much information as it can get on the layout of the rooms, the location of the hostages, and, vitally, clear descriptions of the hostage takers – their personalities, any weapons they may have and so on. This information will also be gained by bugging the building.

Building mock-ups

To make sure that the assault teams know the layout of the building exactly, a full-scale mock-up of the rooms inside is also a likely option. This gives the assault teams an invaluable training aid. During the siege of the Iranian Embassy in May 1980, for example, the SAS built a model of the 50-room building and studied it closely. They also interviewed the caretaker of the Embassy for additional information. The idea is to give the teams so much detailed information about the situation inside the building that once inside

they will be able to go for the gunmen, and the hostages, almost on instinct. With guns being held to the heads of unarmed civilians, the teams just don't have time to find their way around as they go along.

Maximising surprise

If a military rescue is ordered, then the SAS will seek every possible advantage over the terrorists that it can get. This means that if an assault goes in, then it will be timed to hit the gunmen when they are at their lowest ebb. When they are tired, hungry, or disorganised. The best times for this are either very early on in a siege – before the terrorists have had a chance to consolidate their positions – or after several days of siege when they will be very close to exhaustion.

The number of soldiers in a rescue is also

Above: Assault teams will use special lightweight ladders to get through first- and second-floor windows. Below: The last thing an armed terrorist would see when the SAS teams bursts through the door during a rescue.

Above: Pump-action shotguns are sometimes used by SAS teams to blow off door locks. Left: When clearing a building SAS soldiers work in teams. While one moves the others give cover and so on.

carefully thought out. It is governed by the number of rooms to be checked, and the number of entry points to the building. The operation must not be swamped with men, though. When going in, it is reckoned you need to place two men in a room simultaneously; any more than that and members of the team might start shooting one another by mistake.

The start of the assault

The first problem with regard to a hostage-rescue is, of course, getting into the building. Knowing where the hostages are being held will be the governing factor. The assault teams will try to get into the building as close to the hostages as possible – speed is important. If they can enter a building right on top of the hostages, so much the better.

The assault will start with a big diversion to confuse the terrorists, using stun grenades or CS gas. The teams will then force an entry, breaking into the building with sledgehammers, crow bars, hydraulic jacks, bolt cutters, or small battering rams – anything that will get the job done. They are not subtle methods, but at this stage subtlety is a luxury no one can afford. Once inside, doors will be dealt with using the 12-gauge Remington 870 shotgun loaded with a Hatton round – a solid slug which can smash through a door hinge in a second. Explosives are

Above: An SAS soldier equipped for hostage-rescue missions. His main weapon is the Heckler & Koch MP5 submachine gun, which can throw out bullets at a rate of 900 rounds per minute. On his hip is a High Power pistol.

avoided, though, because the blast inside an enclosed room could be dangerous to the people you are trying to save.

Going into a room where hostages and gunmen are together, the object of the SAS rescue operation is to identify the enemy target before the room is even entered. Being able to distinguish between a hostage and a terrorist is a matter of life and death: you are going into a room where you know there is an armed man waiting to kill you. You therefore have to act fast, and act first.

Room clearing

When going into a room, the SAS soldier will go for a position where he has a wide arc of fire, and a protected back. A shouted warning will be given to the hostages to get down, and from then on target identification will be almost instinctive. If he hasn't already recognised the gunmen by sight, then the SAS soldier will shoot anyone still on their feet, anyone in the least bit threatening, and, of course, any-

one armed. He will use sustained and heavy firepower to put down targets, using his 9mm Heckler & Koch MP5 submachine gun or Browning High Power pistol.

Hostage evacuation

With the gunmen dealt with, the next step is to get the remaining people outside for proper identification. Since no one will be absolutely sure who is a hostage and who isn't (at the Iranian Embassy some of the terrorists tried to hide among the hostages), everyone is bound with plastic flexi-cuffs before being led outside. Since the terrorists may be hiding among the hostages, and may even have planted weapons on them, everyone is suspect, and they are all subjected to prisoner handling until vetted. As well as protecting the hostages, binding everyone means no one can shoot any SAS team members. Only then, and only when the building has been properly searched, is the Regiment's hostage-rescue task reckoned to be complete. The SAS team will then disappear quickly to avoid any unwelcome attention from the media.

EYEWITNESS

The Iranian Embassy
5 May 1980

'The cellars were clear. I was now conscious of the sweat. My mouth was dry and I could feel the blood pulsing through my temples. And then we were off again, no time to stop now, up the cellar stairs and into the Embassy reception area. As we advanced across the hallway, there was smoke, confusion, a tremendous clamour of noise coming from above us. The rest of the lads had stormed over the balcony at the front and blasted their way into the first floor of the building with a well-placed explosive charge.'

Soldier 'I'

SELECTION: THE FIRST THREE

SAS Selection is the toughest course in the world. It is simple, brutal and takes no prisoners. The drop-out rate is a phenomenal 96 per cent. But the SAS only wants the cream.

To become an SAS soldier an individual has to pass many hurdles. The first, and probably the hardest, is Selection Training. It is held twice a year – once in the summer, once in the winter – on the wind-swept hills of South Wales. And it lasts four weeks (a three-week build-up and Test Week).

The SAS has no system of direct entry, unlike other special forces units in the world. So how do you put yourself forward for four weeks of personal hell? First of all, you have to volunteer yourself for Selection. The decision rests entirely with the individual. The only condition is that the volunteer must have a minimum of three years' service left from the date that, if successful, he passes Selection Training. This being the case, most men who put themselves forward tend to be in their mid-20s, although individuals have been known to pass Selection as young as 18.

The hunt for recruits

Up until the beginning of 1992, only members of the British Army could volunteer for the SAS, but now men from the Navy, Air Force and Royal Marines are also eligible. The SAS is always under strength, and therefore must cast the net wider for recruits. As an SAS instructor states: 'We now have to go out and tell the Army and the rest of the forces what the SAS is all about in order to attract recruits.'

Many men put themselves forward for Selection each year – around 140 on each course is normal – but few make the grade. Why do they do it?

Reasons for volunteering

A desire to be the best, to be a part of what is reckoned to be the best in the world, is what motivates some. Then there are those who think that being an SAS soldier is the ultimate 'buzz', an irresistible mix of excitement and danger.

For those who have decided that the SAS is for them, the first step is to put in for a Defence Council Instruction (DCI) paper, in which the volunteer certifies that he is prepared to be put for-

ward for 'arduous duties', parachuting and so on. Up until the 1980s, other regiments in the British Army took a dim view of the SAS, believing it 'stole' their best recruits. There is some truth in this. A member of SAS Training Wing admitted that the Regiment 'poached the cream', that they were always on the lookout for the 'good 25-year-old corporal'. Therefore, many volunteers had their applications mysteriously delayed, or were refused permission to volunteer. This has now stopped. However, parent units can still deter men from volunteering for Selection, but in a positive way. They can offer men promotion as an inducement to staying – many accept.

Above: Selection is all about keeping going when your feet are bloody and sore and your lungs are red-raw. Only those with supreme willpower will be able to hack it.

WEEKS

Left: What every man who puts himself forward for Selection wants: the SAS Winged Dagger badge and beige beret. It is the most highly prized item of military headgear in the world bar none. Few get to wear it.

The majority of volunteers – around 70 per cent – come from the Parachute Regiment. Paras are always looking for adventure. They are fit, motivated and aggressive, trained to tackle anything they come up against. For many Paras the SAS is the next logical step.

What the SAS wants

Qualities looked for in recruits include motivation and determination, physical and mental stamina, initiative, self discipline, compatibility for small-group, long-term isolated missions, and the ability to assimilate a wide range of fighting skills. There are two other qualities looked for, though they are not to be found in any Ministry of Defence or SAS handbook. They are a sense of humour and humility. Without these qualities a man will not get through Selection.

There is no way of knowing if a man has these qualities just by looking at him. The instructors know this: 'You can see what's on the outside, but more important is what's within. Only Selection will show what a man's truly made of.'

The start of the course

For those volunteers who turn up at Hereford train station to begin Selection, there is uncertainty. No one knows what to expect. The attitude of the instructors is helpful, though not overly encouraging. The men arrive on a Saturday morning, and are taken straight to Stirling Lines, the SAS's UK base. They are given a medical and then each man must pass the British Army's Battle Fitness Test (this entails covering 2.5km [1.6 miles] in 13 minutes in full kit in a group, then completing the same distance solo in 11.5 minutes). Around 10 per cent fail, and are on their way home immediately.

Once on base the remaining applicants are issued with everything they will need for the next four weeks: boots, bergens (backpacks), webbing,

Left: A soldier in the Brecons struggles up a hillside with a heavy bergen and an SLR. If it rains the bergen will get heavier as the material soaks up the water. And the going will get tougher as the ground becomes wet and slippery.

Above: The men are taken to and from the hills in the four-tonners. In the mornings they try to get some sleep during the journey, but the wind gets in the back and chills them to the bone. This means they are tired before the work on the hills begins.

uniforms and de-activated Self-Loading Rifles (SLRs). Much of the kit is old. This is deliberate. The webbing and bergens soak up any wet, making them heavier. This results in bergen sores and blisters. Ill-fitting boots result in painful foot blisters. All this is designed to test motivation.

The men are then taken to Dering Lines, a battle school based in Brecon. For the next four weeks this will be their home (it was felt that they should only be based at Stirling Lines when they are fully fledged SAS soldiers). The quarters are comfortable, and the food is hot and ample.

The first week

The first Sunday marks the start of the course. This is the beginning of the first week. The exercises the men have to perform over the next four weeks do not change. They consist of timed navigation marches over the Brecon Beacons, with each man having to reach pre-arranged rendezvous (RV) points along his route. The only things that increase are the loads he has to carry, and the distances he has to travel. The routes are set by the training staff, and there are instructors at each RV to check on the progress of each volunteer, as well as to make sure that no one is

Right: Selection is held twice a year: once in the summer, once in the winter. On winter Selection there isn't the searing heat. But there is a risk of hypothermia due to the freezing wind.

Above: A group on SAS Selection in the 1960s. Apart from the Lee-Enfield rifles, very little has changed. Why should it? It is an excellent test of suitability for the SAS.

Below: Each man on Selection has an equal chance. He is given a map, a compass and the grid reference of the first rendezvous (RV). When he gets there he will be told the next RV, and so on. All the time he is being assessed.

breaking the rules. The rules are simple: everyone has the same weight on his back, and everyone has to complete each course in the allotted time.

The men turf out of bed at around 0400 hours, have breakfast, and then it's into the trucks for the journey to the Brecon Beacons. The Beacons are subject to driving rain, sleet and snow, high winds, and they have little natural cover.

SAS 'Sickeners'

When they arrive they are sorted into groups. This is only for organisational purposes. They are really on their own. Each man's bergen is weighed and inspected – no one starts with an unfair advantage. Even at this stage the instructors will have noted those they want to get rid of. In the past they used so-called 'Sickeners' to get rid of men who weren't the right material. These consisted of making volunteers crawl through ditches filled with sheep's entrails, or pulling a Land Rover up the side of a hill with ropes, then letting it roll back down, after which it would have to be hauled up again, and so on. Other 'Sickeners' involved carrying rocks from RV to RV, or having to remove boot laces halfway through a march, which would result in large blisters and swollen feet. The 'Sickener factor' has now gone, but the instructors still get rid of those considered unsuitable as quickly as possible.

Then the groups head for the hills. Though the distances may not seem that great, at least at first – they start at around 10km (6.25 miles) – the men have to travel up and down steep gradients, map-reading all the time to ensure they get to each RV. And they are carrying 18kg (40lb) on their backs, plus their personal weapon – another 4.45kg (10lb) – which has no sling. One who took part in

a 10km (6.25-mile) speed march remembers the pain: 'The pace of marches is crippling. For me the worst was the 10km speed march with bergen, belt order and weapon. The pain in my legs and hips will always be with me. My whole body was on fire, but I knew I couldn't give in.'

The use of roads is strictly forbidden. They are only allowed to walk along animal tracks and Roman roads. Anyone caught cheating is failed. The marches are made worse by the weather, as one volunteer remembers: 'You can start off in bright sunshine but after an hour or so it will suddenly get cloudy and cold. Then you get to the top of a ridge and the driving rain will tear into you, stinging your eyes and buffeting your body.'

Increasing the pressure

The marches increase in length, up to 20km (12.5 miles) and beyond. And the pressure is on all the time, as an SAS instructor states: 'It's all down to time. The trick is to go flat out to get A grades on the easy marches. If you can march 20km (12.5 miles) in three hours and 20 minutes you get an A grade, if you do it in three hours 30 minutes you get a B grade. The grading is very tight.' Failing one exercise does not necessarily mean failing the course. If a man fails a march because of poor map-reading, he will stay on the course if he achieved A grades in his previous marches.

The culmination of the first week is the High Walk, a 23km (14-mile) hill-walking exercise in the Brecons. Movement is again in groups, but it is individuals who are timed. It has to be completed in four hours and 10 minutes in good weather. If conditions are poor, additional time is allowed to complete the course. Each man carries just over 18kg (40lb) on his body, plus his rifle. He is also given a map with the designated RVs marked on.

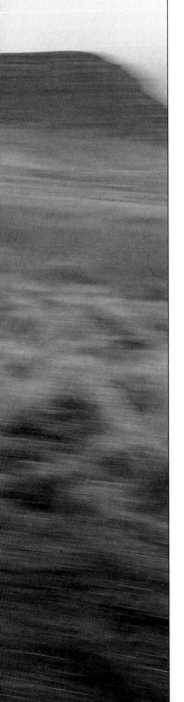

GOOD POINTS

✔ Selection is a very cost-effective way of sorting out soldiers who have SAS potential, and the abolition of the Sickener factor has shifted the emphasis from discouragement to encouragement.

✔ Selection is still rated as one of the best initial special forces training courses in the world.

✔ Volunteers can attempt Selection a number of times (up to half a dozen), giving those who suffer injuries on the course another chance.

BAD POINTS

✘ The hard physical nature of Selection can result in some long-term knee and ankle injuries in individuals, which can damage careers.

✘ There are only two Selection courses a year, which means the SAS's annual intake of recruits (usually around 12-15) is insufficient to meet the Regiment's manpower requirements.

✘ Selection is still viewed with suspicion by many units in the British Army, Navy and Air Force.

After a full week of marching on the hills, everyone is tired. Many men's feet are cut to ribbons and are heavily bandaged. Others have large bergen burns on their backs. Tendons and ligaments are aching, and everyone's body is tired.

Nevertheless, from the SAS's point of view the first week is the 'easy bit', and it has got rid of the unsuitable. The 'wasters' (those who just wanted a break from mundane Army life), the 'lambs' (those whose fitness was poor), and the ones who are a 'mouth on a stick' (those who are loud and whose character does not fit the Regiment) will have gone. The committed remain, though even some of these will have quit because of injuries.

Once the High Walk is over, there follows a further two weeks of navigation exercises and physical training. The men are out on the hills during the day and in the classrooms in the evening. Each man is now getting an average of four hours' sleep a night, and the strain is beginning to tell. Tired bodies and minds result in lethargy and irritability. All this is carefully noted by the staff of Training Wing. If a man loses his sense of humour after only two weeks of graft, he is no good to the SAS.

Pushed to the limits

The physical pace is hard, though keeping up mental stamina is just as hard. For example, when individuals reach certain RVs they may be given a foreign weapon to strip and re-assemble. The SAS needs men who can think even when they are physically exhausted. There is no shouting or encouragement from the instructors, just a constant monitoring.

For those who are still left on Selection Training after three weeks, the greatest challenge is yet to come. All that went before was just a build-up, a preparation for the biggest test most of them will face in their lives: the hell of Test Week.

Below: For some it is too much, and they have to be given help. A number of men have died on the hills due to hypothermia or exhaustion. This is a heavy price to pay to keep standards up.

SELECTION: TEST WEEK

It has killed men, reduced others to wheelchair-bound cripples and inflicted so much pain on some that they have vowed never to tackle Selection again. Welcome to Test Week, the Special Air Service's own version of hell on earth.

Selection is all about pain, both physical and mental, and overcoming it. There is no room for sentiment when it comes to choosing who is suitable for the Special Air Service. And the most brutal hurdle on Selection is Test Week.

Test Week is very simple. It consists of six hill-walking exercises in the Elan Valley and Brecon Beacons in South Wales. The first five marches progress in length from 25 to 28km (15-17 miles), with the weight carried by each man also increasing from 20.4kg (45lb) to 25kg (55lb), in addition to his personal weapon – a Self-Loading Rifle (SLR). The final march is the culmination of Test Week, and Selection: the Endurance March. It is a 64km (40-mile) solo march which has to be completed in 20 hours. It is a killer, pure and simple.

By Test Week most of the original intake has failed or voluntarily withdrawn from the course. There are only around 25 or 30 left of the original 140. Only the dedicated are left, but even for these the task ahead is daunting. A recent Ministry of

Far left: Test Week is hard, unbelievably hard. Men have to push themselves through the pain barrier to succeed. Below: On the barren Brecon Beacons, map-reading skills are crucial.

Defence memorandum concerning SAS Selection stated that volunteers during Test Week 'must average a consistent 4km (2.5 miles) per hour under good weather conditions to pass the test marches'. Over flat terrain this would be relatively easy, but over the hills of the Brecons it is a blistering pace.

No pain, no gain

It is made worse by the fact that all the men's minds and bodies are tired. During the previous three weeks they have been pushed to their physical and mental limits. Limbs and feet are sore and often bloodied, and some of the men are carrying severe knee and ankle injuries.

To make things more difficult, during the early marches on Test Week the men have to swim the River Wye carrying their bergens, weapons and clothes. They also have to go up and down the highest mountain in the area three times. Pen-y-Fan is 900m (3000ft) high and has steep slopes. Sounds easy? For someone loaded down with an 18kg (40lb) bergen, belt order and a personal weapon with no sling, it is a fearsome obstacle. Each man must jog to keep up his times, navigating from one rendezvous (RV) to the next, with no motivation or companionship from others.

Rules on the hills

To pass Test Week physical fitness is not enough. A man must have mental toughness as well. He must ignore the pain he is feeling, and concentrate on getting to the next RV. As one who went through Test Week states: 'It's all about keeping your mind working, you see. Those who don't use their initiative fall back and fail.'

The instructors ensure each man is alone during the marches. If two men are caught walking together they are failed. The sense of isolation can also be increased by the weather. The area is subject to changeable conditions, and if the cloud closes in a man can feel totally alone. Rain can also add to the misery: 'it rained continuously when I did Test Week, rained every day. We did not have waterproof clothing, so we stayed wet all the time. We came home at night and tried to dry out our clothes, but they were still damp in the morning.'

Increasing the pace

The staff of Training Wing who are on the hills make sure the volunteers keep up the pace. When a man gets to an RV there is no encouragement from them, just frantic urgings for him to get to the next RV. The attitude of some instructors can add to the misery. An SAS veteran who ran Training Wing explains: 'Those instructors who

Below: On top of the 'Fan'. Clambering up and down this steep-sided hill can wreck knees, ankles and potential SAS careers. The worst thing about Pen-y-Fan is the weather. It's always windy and prone to heavy rain.

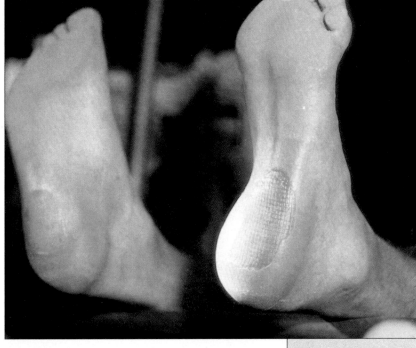

Above: What does it take to pass Test Week? The ability to ignore foot injuries like these for one. You have to be able to bind them, put your boots on and get back on the hills. Every step feels like you're walking on hot coals. But if you want to be an SAS soldier you have to train your mind to ignore such things.
Right: Tired, hungry and wet, and still a long way to go.

had a hard time of it themselves on Selection don't want anyone to pass. They see the volunteers as a threat. This being the case, a streak of cruelty comes out in them. I had to make sure that everyone was given a fair crack of the whip.'

That said, men are rarely failed by instructors on Test Week – they fail themselves. An instructor explains: 'It's a self-selecting process on Test Week. They fail themselves. They come to an RV and say "I can't go on." I then make it quite clear what they are doing, and ask them if they really want to be pulled off the course. It's a bit pathetic. They just nod their heads as they stare at the ground.' Why do they fail themselves? 'Essentially it's because they are exhausted. Either that or they have leg injuries.'

The instructors know that the course exacts a heavy toll on men's bodies, but they are also aware that volunteers can use the excuse of an injury to quit. They then claim that the injury forced them to quit, when the real reason was lack of determination. The medical officer's door is never closed. Be it late at night or early in the morning, volunteers are free to go and get themselves checked out. Again the instructors are watching. 'Some blokes would go to the MO

Above: Some men suffer injuries that force them to quit. This is not necessarily the end, but they will have to wait until the next Selection to get another crack. However, the injuries some suffer are so bad that they will never walk properly again, let alone be able to tackle Selection.

[Medical Officer] at night with their feet in ribbons, but they would be there in the line-up the next morning, ready to go out onto the hills. That's the sort of attitude we're looking for. You get points for trying, you see. If they give in you can't help them.'

Common injuries

Surprisingly, the majority of injuries are not twisted ankles or knees but blisters and bergen sores. There are leg injuries, of course, but there are also back problems and men suffering from piles.

Those who can keep their minds working have an easier time of it on Test Week. One who passed remembers one of the tricks he pulled: 'You can cheat on the hills if you keep your wits about you.

The easiest way is to fill up your pack with water. When you get to the RV your pack is weighed and is the correct weight. After you have left the RV you can let some of the water out to make it lighter. But you have to remember to try and fill it before you get to the next RV. It's all about keeping the grey matter working, you see.' Prospective volunteers beware: the instructors have got wise to this trick and now inspect all bergens at regular intervals between RVs.

The culmination of Test Week is the Endurance March, nicknamed the 'Fan Dance' or 'Long Drag'. It is difficult enough, but is made worse by the fact that the men are already fatigued by the previous marches. This cuts no ice with the instructors. The volunteers have to cover the 64km (40 miles) in the allotted time. Each man carries 25kg (55lb) on his back, plus his weapon. Equipped with map, compass and the grid reference of the first RV, he sets off alone.

The author of *Soldier 'I'* was one of those

Above and below: Pen-y-Fan is not the highest mountain in the world, but to those who have to tackle it during Test Week it seems like Mount Everest. The men have to dig deep to conquer it, but conquer it they must to become one of the elite.

who took part, and he provides a graphic account of the Endurance March: 'Midday. I'd been going for eight hours and I reckoned I was still less than halfway round the course. The sun was extraordinarily hot for the time of year... As I paused momentarily to get my bearings, my legs began to give way under the load of the bergen. My lungs felt raw, as if someone had thrust their fist down my throat and ripped a layer of skin off them.' Each man has to make all the RVs in the time allowed. If he doesn't he fails.

Death on the hills

Some men get lost on the hills, and have to spend the night out in the open. As well as failing the march, and Selection, they risk the danger of hypothermia if it's a winter course. The contents of their bergens will help them survive until they are found, but the SAS does not worry unduly that men may die on Selection. To the SAS this is the price that has to be paid for keeping up standards of excellence.

How many are left at the end of Test Week? The answer is very few. On average, around 200 men apply for each Selection course. Of these, a quarter withdraw prior to the start of the course.

standard operating procedures (SOPs), such as how to move through hostile territory as part of a four-man patrol. The attitude of the instructors undergoes a change: they are helpful. After all, the volunteers are SAS potential now.

Each student receives instruction in SAS patrols skills and combat and survival training, where they learn how to live off the land. Combat and survival includes a resistance-to-interrogation exercise. Many crack at this stage, and are RTU'd.

Those who pass then go on to complete jungle training and a static-line parachute course. They can be RTU'd on the last day of the parachute course, so they have to keep up their concentration to the end. After completing all the courses, those who remain are awarded their Winged Dagger badges. They are now SAS soldiers.

Below: Test Week is the worst part of Selection, and the Endurance March the hardest part of Test Week. Only five or six out of 140 get this far. The march is made worse by the sense of isolation each man experiences. As one who took part remembers: 'I was overwhelmed by feelings of loneliness. I felt as though I was the only person for miles around.'

GOOD POINTS

✔ Test Week is the most effective way of determining who has what it takes to be an SAS soldier.

✔ It is extremely simple and fair. Everyone starts with the same weight of equipment and amount of clothing.

✔ It has contributed to maintaining the SAS's standards of excellence over the past 40 years.

✔ It is relatively short, which means it is not expensive to run in terms of manpower and money.

BAD POINTS

✗ Test Week is probably the most brutal course in the world in terms of demands put on individuals. It can physically break experienced soldiers.

✗ It has led to several deaths on the Brecon Beacons, especially on 'Long Drag'.

✗ The nature of Test Week has resulted in many long-term and irreversible leg and knee injuries among volunteers.

✗ The final part of Selection has psychologically destroyed many fine men.

Therefore, approximately 140-150 men start each Selection. During the first three weeks over 100 will either fail to achieve the pass times for the marches and will be returned to their units (RTU'd), or will voluntarily withdraw from the course. At the end of Test Week only five or six will be judged suitable to go on to Continuation Training, the next stage of the SAS's recruitment course. This represents an overall attrition rate of over 95 per cent for each Selection.

Those who pass Selection will attend Continuation Training. It lasts around four months and is far less strenuous than Selection. The volunteers learn basic SAS skills. They are taught

JUNGLE WARFARE

SAS jungle warfare training has one aim: to ensure that the Regiment's men are faster and more accurate with their weapons than the enemy. This means learning the Regiment's tried and tested standard operating procedures.

Above: Contacts in the jungle are always at close range – there is no place to hide. Only those with quick reflexes and better weapons skills will survive. That is why the SAS usually wins.

Jungle warfare skills are first taught to prospective SAS troopers during the jungle training phase that takes place immediately after Continuation Training (see p.54). Once they are serving in their Sabre Squadrons, however, all SAS soldiers will receive refresher courses when their unit is deployed to the Far East or Central America. SAS jungle warfare skills are based on simple principles: that thorough training, planning and preparation saves lives.

The nature of jungle fighting

SAS jungle training courses last four weeks and include survival skills (one week), navigation (one week) and warfare tactics (two weeks). The warfare part of the course stresses silent movement and ace weapons skills.

Firefights in the jungle take place at close range – around 5m (17ft) – and involve small groups. Noise discipline is crucial to staying alive, especially when moving through dense jungle where visibility is poor. An SAS four-man patrol does not hack its way through the trees. It moves silently and stealthily at a rate of 100m (328ft) an hour, sometimes slower. Every 20 minutes the whole patrol stops and listens for possible pursuers.

Unseen enemies

As well as watching for the enemy, each SAS man takes great care where he steps. He has to watch for twigs and dried leaves, which will make a cracking sound if stepped on. He will also have to watch out for snakes, and scorpions, ants' and spiders' nests. He can't let his concentration slip for a second. In the sapping humidity of the jungle this type of work calls for a special kind of soldier.

To be a jungle fighter an SAS soldier has to be supremely fit. Wading through a swamp for hours on end, carrying a rifle above your head, is a severe test of physical fitness. Even out of the water you get wet through sweating continuously.

The humidity means fluid loss is very high. And it is increased by each man having to carry up to 36kg (80lb) on his back, enough to sustain him for 14 days in the jungle. But being able to move through the jungle is not enough – SAS soldiers must be able to fight among the trees.

Above: Getting across a river the SAS way – guns at the ready.
Below: Jungle patrolling demands maximum concentration.

Above: A New Zealand SAS trooper goes through the drills for firing an assault rifle from the hip.
Left: A suspicious sound is heard. He has a split-second to bring his weapon to bear. It's just a training exercise on this occasion, but next time it might be for real.

Movement and fighting rules are enshrined in SAS standard operating procedures (SOPs). These are taught to troopers until they become second nature. They include some simple rules: do not use tracks, paths or rivers to travel along. They will either be booby-trapped or contain an enemy ambush. Give villages and other habitated areas a wide berth.

Training stresses the importance of avoiding using foliage as camouflage. It may seem like a good idea to cut branches and leaves off trees and bushes and stick them on webbing and headgear. However, as soon as it is cut, foliage starts dying and fading. It then contrasts sharply with its lush surroundings, making patrol members stick out like sore thumbs.

The instructors stress SOPs to the men over and over again: patrols have to move silently, which means moving slowly. You're better slow than dead. Similarly, they will hammer home the message that holding ground in a contact is definitely not an SOP. Instead, contact drills revolve around the ability to lay down a lot of instantaneous fire to allow the patrol to escape.

Contact drills

The contact drills taught in training are the result of hard-learned lessons in Malaya in the 1950s and Borneo in the 1960s. In jungle SAS four-man patrols move in file, one man behind the other. When contact is made with the enemy, it is always the trooper at the front, the lead scout, who makes contact first. Therefore, the SAS head-on contact drill was devised. When a contact happens the other patrol members are trained to move into positions either side of the lead scout to pour fire at the enemy. In this way four men are firing at the enemy instead of one. But the head-on contact drill is only one part of the equation. The other part is the SOP known as 'shoot and scoot'.

Shoot and scoot

Shoot and scoot was invented by Lieutenant-Colonel John Woodhouse, an SAS veteran of Malaya. It is simple: after laying down a barrage of fire, the SAS patrol splits up and heads for an emergency rendezvous, each man taking a different route. As a method of getting away fast and avoiding casualties it is superb.

But for these tactics to work, SAS soldiers have to learn to fire their weapons properly. As a result, weapon skills are the most important part of jungle training. SAS soldiers can only become effective jungle fighters if their personal weapons become an integral part of themselves, almost like an extension of their bodies. This being the case, the choice of weapons is crucial.

SAS soldiers prefer the M16 assault rifle in the jungle. The weapon is light, which means it is easy to bring to bear in a firefight, and it has little recoil, which makes it both easy and comfortable to fire. That said, almost all modern assault rifles are lightweight and compact, making them ideal for jungle warfare.

In the jungle SAS soldiers have to learn instinctive point firing. This means carrying their personal weapons in a different way. Each man holds his weapon in his hands – there are no rifle slings. The butt is always in the shoulder so the rifle is always ready to bring to bear. The index finger – the trigger finger – is always resting on the trigger

guard. Each men leans into his weapon, a position that makes firing much easier.

Instinctive point stresses that troopers must shoot only when a target is visible: wild firing only wastes ammunition. Both eyes remain open. The instructors teach the men how to pivot to fire at a target. It is no good swinging to fire, they are told, you will miss. When they open fire SAS soldiers always use the double tap (two shots fired in quick succession). Between the first and second shot a trooper must make an adjustment to ensure that the second round is dead on target.

Weapons must work first time every time, and so the course devotes a great deal of time to weapons maintenance. The jungle is humid. Everything goes rusty very quickly without proper care. Troopers thus have to clean their weapons several times a day, and make sure they are oiled. However, there is a problem with oil, as a member of Training Wing explains: 'If you oil the barrel,

Top: A motley crew! These scruffy individuals are the skilled men who teach jungle warfare tactics. These are from the jungle school in Brunei. Above: An SAS man must plan each step carefully. If he steps on a dry twig, the crack will seem like a thunderclap and may be heard by an enemy patrol.

Above: Weapon into the shoulder, forefinger on the trigger – ready for anything. The men's weapons skills are honed to perfection on the jungle course, but it is also impressed upon them that it is important to keep rifles and machine guns well oiled and functional. Weapons are cleaned daily, and magazines are changed every five days to ensure their springs keep working properly. A firefight is over in seconds – the first shot counts.

and don't dry-clean it before you shoot, the first round you fire will go high because it will be tight in the barrel. Also, it will produce a lot of smoke, which can give away your position in an ambush.'

Though weapons are cleaned every day, they are not cleaned at the same time: three out of four weapons are always loaded and ready to fire. Also, SAS SOPs demand that each patrol member has his weapon within arm's reach at all times.

Magazines can be a problem with regard to stoppages. Training therefore stresses the importance of their maintenance. As well as keeping them clean, they must be changed frequently to keep their springs working, as the instructors stress time and time again.

The M16's magazine takes 30 rounds, but SAS soldiers will only load them with 29. In this way the magazine's spring is not fully compressed. If a

Above: Travelling on rivers in the jungle is not encouraged, but if there is no alternative the boats are camouflaged.

Above: Say cheese! Another SAS jungle warfare course ends with the mandatory group photograph.

magazine has 30 rounds and it is full over a long period, the spring will be too weak to operate properly. Improper feeding of rounds into the chamber can cause a stoppage – potentially fatal in a firefight. Every five days, therefore, the magazine is taken out of the weapon, the rounds are extracted and put in a fresh magazine, which is then loaded into the weapon.

The popular image of elite troops is that they are armed to the teeth with a multitude of weapons. This could not be further from the truth. SAS soldiers in the jungle carry only one weapon – there's no point in carrying around different types of ammunition.

Jungle training, like most skills taught to members of the Regiment, never stops in the SAS. Soldiers are given regular refresher courses throughout their careers to ensure they are up to speed. But how good is the training they receive? SAS soldiers have been operating in jungles for nearly 50 years. During that time not one single SAS patrol has been wiped out in an ambush – testimony to the effectiveness of SOPs.

GOOD POINTS

✔ SAS jungle warfare skills are acknowledged by other elite units as being the best in the world.

✔ Jungle warfare specialists such as the New Zealand and Australian SAS cross-train with their British counterparts.

✔ SAS jungle warfare tactics have won two wars: in Malaya in the 1950s and Borneo in the 1960s.

✔ Because of the small size of classes, SAS instructors can provide more in-depth training for individuals.

BAD POINTS

✘ The SAS has not fought a jungle war for 30 years. Many feel that training cannot make up for lack of the real thing.

✘ Two weeks is not long enough to master all SAS standard operating procedures as they apply to jungle warfare.

✘ SAS soldiers are spending less and less time in the jungle as a result of other priorities within the Regiment.

✘ British defence cuts in general will affect the SAS's jungle warfare training facilities in the future.

COMBAT MEDICINE

The patrol medic is the most important member of an SAS four-man patrol. On operations he can treat himself, the other members of the patrol and the locals as part of the SAS's 'hearts and minds' strategy. Medical training is therefore very important in the Regiment.

Above: A surgical team from 5 Airborne Brigade carries out an operation on a soldier with a severe stomach wound. SAS men are trained how to perform similar operations on their medical courses. This is because SAS units operate deep inside enemy territory, far away from friendly hospital facilities.

The SAS four-man patrol is a self-contained unit: it can operate on its own and contains a combination of skills that allows it to fight at maximum effectiveness. This is because each man in the patrol has his own patrol skill, although normally a patrol member will be trained in two or more patrol skills.

SAS patrol skills are signalling, demolitions, medicine and languages. Of these, the most important is medicine. Because the Regiment's units often fight deep behind enemy lines, far from friendly bases and hospitals, SAS soldiers have to be their own doctors, able to treat themselves and other members of the patrol. In addition, medical

skills are also important to the SAS's 'hearts and minds' concept (the belief that by gaining the trust and respect of local inhabitants SAS soldiers will win them over; medical treatment is an effective way of doing this). In Malaya, Borneo and Oman, for example, the locals were often won over to the SAS's cause by patrol medics setting up makeshift surgeries to treat their ailments – it was remarkable what a few aspirins could achieve.

With medicine therefore being so important to the Regiment's art of war, medical training in the SAS starts early. At the start of Selection Training, the first phase of SAS recruitment, even before they have joined the Regiment, the men are briefed on

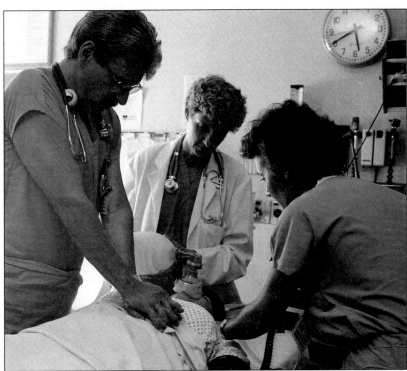

stroke and heat exhaustion. The men will also be taught how to treat snake bites, a wise precaution as part of the course involves jungle training in the Far East. All this is really just scratching the surface, though: comprehensive medical training begins once a man is a fully fledged SAS soldier.

The Regiment takes medical skills very seriously, and therefore ensures its soldiers receive intensive training in all aspects of the preservation of life. This may sound contradictory; after all, SAS soldiers are usually the ones dealing out death and destruction. However, it is all part of being complete elite specialists.

The medical course

Medical skills are taught on a 12-week course run at Stirling Lines in Hereford, the SAS's UK base. The first eight weeks are filled with intensive classroom work. Forget the idea of soldiers only learning how to stitch up wounds or give the kiss of life – this course is mentally demanding and covers everything. The students are taught all there is to know about physiology and anatomy. For men who have probably never studied medicine in their lives this is a tough task, but one that they must master in order to become fully rounded SAS soldiers.

The course is run by Training Wing, 22 SAS, but the instructors are attached doctors from the Royal Army Medical Corps. Under their supervision the SAS soldiers learn a whole range of medical skills, everything from how to give injections and administer drugs to treating gunshot wounds and amputating limbs.

Above: Resuscitating a patient in cardiac arrest in an NHS casualty department, the kind of problem an SAS man on medical training might have to deal with. SAS soldiers serve four-week hospital attachments during their medical training, but only after they have convinced the hospital authorities that they are up to scratch. The attachments add a degree of realism and pressure that tests whether an SAS soldier will make a good patrol medic.

the dangers of hypothermia – the cooling of the body below its normal temperature of 36-38 degrees C (97-100 degrees F) – and how to treat it. The course is held in the Black Mountains of South Wales, an area known for its extremes of temperature, so this is a sensible precaution.

Medical training during Continuation

During Continuation Training, the second phase of SAS recruitment, those who are left on the course are taught immediate first aid. This includes how to stop bleeding, cardiopulmonary resuscitation (CPR) – keeping a patient's heart beating – the effects of climate on the body, and how to treat heat

Top: On the medical course the students will learn how to administer injections and set up drips.
Above: A doctor treats a soldier's badly blistered feet. Being able to treat foot injuries is an essential part of SAS medical training, especially as marching is often the main form of travel for SAS four-man patrols.
Right: It's just a simulation here, but many SAS medics will have to perform amputations during their careers, often the result of stepping on a mine.

Above: One of the patrol goes down, shot by an enemy sniper. The SAS medic has seconds to dress the sucking chest wound before the man dies – no problem.
Left: Many soldiers who are wounded in action go into shock, so SAS medics are trained to deal with this.
Below: Gaping leg wounds are not a pretty sight, but SAS medics will see plenty of them during their service lives.

The days on the course are very long, and the men have to give 100 per cent attention at all times. The first week consists of learning all about the human body, muscles, the skeleton and so on. Then the students are introduced to trauma, such as gunshot wounds, puncture wounds and cuts. The men also learn the layout, problems, injuries to and cures for the nose, ears, eyes, heart and lungs. For example, there will be a morning devoted to eyes and how to treat injuries to them.

SAS midwives?

Surprisingly, the men also learn midwifery skills. Being able to treat wounds resultant from being shot or stepping on a mine is obvious, but being able to deliver babies? A member of Training Wing explains: 'Midwifery is part of the "hearts and minds" set-up. In Borneo in the 1960s, for example, some of the clinics that we set up treated up to 400 locals each. They dealt with everything from delivering babies to treating worms and dysentery. We even treated the locals' animals when they were brought in. It was great for establishing trust and

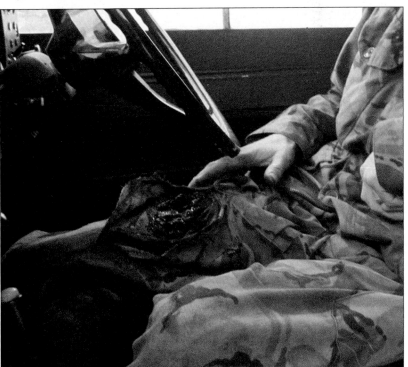

Above: Medical skills are integral to SAS 'hearts and minds' campaigns, whereby SAS soldiers gain the trust of the locals by providing them with free medical aid. In the 1960s SAS soldiers won over the locals in Borneo (inset) and during the 1980s and 1990s they did the same in Belize (main picture).

picking up bits of information through the local grapevine.'

The last four weeks of the course consist of hospital attachments. Before they go, though, the students have to prove they are up to paramedic standard – National Health Service hospitals will only accept SAS personnel if they are up to scratch. During the previous eight weeks the men may have been giving themselves injections and treating injured members of the SAS squadrons under supervision at Stirling Lines, but attachment to a casualty department of a local hospital adds a degree of realism. The pressure is also increased, which tests their confidence and patience.

On casualty attachment

In general the students cope well, their keen minds having absorbed the knowledge taught to them during the previous eight weeks – very few fail to make the grade.

The students also begin to appreciate the value of what is being taught to them: that they, like the Regiment, will become self-sufficient. This makes the men want to learn. An instructor explains: 'Medical knowledge is a very important aspect of an SAS four-man patrol. Guys feel better on operations knowing that everyone knows how to deal with injuries. We have to be our own doctors: in the middle of nowhere there's no one else around. Good medics are essential on operations.'

Perks of the course

Toughened SAS soldiers may seem the last types to be found walking hospital corridors in white uniforms. However, the men enjoy their hospital attachments. A member of B Squadron explains why: 'When you go on hospital attachment you get extra money allowances. Also, there's a lot of nurses and they love SAS soldiers. This means most of the guys get plenty of bonking practice in.' This being the case, there is no shortage of volunteers for medical courses. In addition, there is the matter of promotion – passing medical training is essential for career progression within the Regiment.

Keeping up with the missus

For the married members of the Regiment there is a different incentive to succeed at medicine, as one of Training Wing's instructors states: 'A lot of the blokes have nurses for wives, and they want to keep up to scratch with them.' Once the course is over the men go back to their squadrons. However, like many other aspects of training in the SAS, refresher courses are essential, particularly when the soldiers go on deployments. If a squadron is sent to the jungle, for example, its medics will learn all about tropical diseases.

Bush medicine

SAS patrols carry state-of-the-art medicines and equipment in their medical packs on operations, but members of the Regiment also have to be familiar with wilderness medicine. This means learning which plants have therapeutic and healing properties, and such skills as how to make poultices and drugs and so on. An SAS soldier explains: 'It's nice to have all the gear, but every now and then you will be in a position where you have nothing. But you still might have to treat yourself or a wounded comrade. The only things you will have are the plants and herbs growing around you, so you must know bush medicine.'

On operations everyone carries their own medical kits – the patrol medic will only treat serious problems. If an individual has a headache, for example, he will take one of his own pills. But what happens if the patrol medic is killed or seriously injured? 'In the Regiment we believe that cross-training is very important. It's no use having just one bloke in the patrol who knows medicine. If he gets killed the patrol is stuffed. That's the reason for cross-training – the patrol will always have someone to treat injuries.'

The patrol medic

Medical training also covers the responsibilities of the patrol medic. It's not just a case of stitching wounds and mending broken bones. The medic has other vitally important tasks in the field. The lives of the other members of the unit are in his hands. For example, he ensures standards of hygiene are maintained at base camp, he positions the latrines and treats drinking water. He will also be responsible for establishing clinics for the locals where applicable, which may decide the outcome of an SAS 'hearts and minds' campaign.

Given the vital role played by medics, the Regiment always ensures it has enough of them. If there is a shortage in one squadron, for example, then the next batch of recruits will be told they will be patrol medics. Not all are keen initially, as a member of Training Wing explains: 'A lot of the blokes just want to be demolitions experts and blow things to bits. But I tell them it's tough shit – they're going to be medics. In general they make good medics, especially when they learn about the extra pay and the nurses! I've also found that Ruperts [SAS slang for officers] make crap medics, but that's just my opinion.'

Knowing that there will no immediate medical backup on missions acts as an incentive to learn medicine, especially when there's a good chance of getting shot and contracting tropical diseases. And it's a knowledge that is useful later on in life. One ex-SAS soldier says: 'I could carry out amputations in my garden shed if I wanted, and I can also look after my family's health. That makes me feel good.'

Below: A fully stocked medical kit – the sort that SAS patrol medics will take with them on missions. Each patrol member will also be equipped with his own medicines.

STATIC-LINE PARACHUTING

Learning to jump out of an aircraft is an essential part of being an SAS soldier. So parachute training starts early in the Regiment, at RAF Brize Norton.

Above: A static-line parachute drop from a Hercules aircraft. A static-line jump is where the parachute ripcord is pulled automatically when each soldier leaves the aircraft. Potential SAS soldiers attend the static-line course at RAF Brize Norton in Oxfordshire to win their parachute 'wings'.

Before he becomes a fully fledged SAS soldier, a recruit has to pass numerous courses. The final hurdle before he can wear the famous Winged Dagger badge and khaki beret is the static-line parachute course, which is held at RAF Brize Norton in Oxfordshire.

SAS soldiers have to be able to arrive at their targets by land, sea and air. During the course of their careers they will learn all about combat diving and strike vehicles, but from day one all the Regiment's soldiers have to be parachute-trained. Every member of the Sabre Squadrons wears the famous SAS wings on his chest, indicating he is a

parachutist. To win this coveted piece of cloth he has to pass the static-line parachute course.

The course lasts four weeks, and is held at least four times a year. As well as potential SAS soldiers, recruits from The Parachute Regiment also attend. It is run by RAF Parachute Jump Instructors (PJIs), and they teach an average of 30 men on each course.

The aim is very simple: the PJIs teach the recruits how to make a static-line jump from an aircraft. A static-line jump is where the parachute ripcord is pulled automatically when a parachutist jumps from the aircraft. To pass the course, each

that this is the last hurdle they have to pass before they become one of the elite adds to their determination to pass.

But those who think that they will be jumping from an aircraft on day one will be disappointed. The PJIs are among the best in the world at their job. They have to ensure that each man is thoroughly trained and briefed before he can make a jump. Landing on a drop zone (DZ) is fine, but if a soldier is wounded when he lands then he is useless to his unit. The first week, therefore, consists of learning how to make safe parachute landings. And that means starting right at the beginning – on mats in the aircraft hangar.

Below: RAF Hercules long-range transport aircraft line up ready for take-off. The students on the parachute course make eight jumps in all, each one from a Hercules. The aircraft is one of the most rugged military transport aircraft in the world, each capable of off-loading 90 fully equipped paratroopers in one drop.

The first week

Muster is held at 0800 hours (this is like a holiday for the SAS volunteers, who have been used to getting up at 0400 hours). A roll-call is taken and then the course divides into classes (there areusually around 40 students on each course). Then it's into the hangars to practise parachute rolls for an hour, followed by a tea break. Afterwards the class will be lectured about parachute flight techniques, followed by more rolls and aircraft drills, such as how to stand in the door and action-station procedures. After a leisurely lunch there will be more parachute rolls, as well as lectures on the theory of parachutes and the types of aircraft the men will be jumping from. The talks are designed to give the men a rest from the physical exercises, as well as make the day more interesting.

In the hangars the students start on the floor mats. They are taught the proper position for landing: chin on chest, elbows in, legs together, knees

potential SAS soldier must make eight jumps, including one at night. All straightforward stuff. The students themselves usually enjoy Brize Norton, as a serving SAS soldier states: 'I really liked it. The instruction is excellent and the regime is very laidback. The PJIs are coaching you to do things, not shouting at you. It was a good time. What you have to remember is that you've just gone through five months of sheer hell. Then you end up at Brize sleeping in clean sheets and eating good scoff. Heaven!' The relaxed atmosphere and civilised hours are a welcome break for the SAS volunteers, and the fact

bent and feet flat to the floor. They will then practise rolling on the mats: rolling to the right, to the
left, forward and so on.

The week progresses, all the time the PJIs giving encouragement and advice. Halfway through
the week the rolls become more difficult. They are
made from a 1m-high platform. This is in fact a
very effective way of correcting bad stances.
Those who have poor stances or are sloppy feel
aches and pains, and improve their techniques.

Flight drills

The PJIs then introduce the men to flight drills;
the procedures they will follow when making a
real jump, such as looking up immediately after
the 'chute opens to check their canopy. If their rig
lines are twisted they will have to untangle them.
In the hangar they are taught how to do this. There
are many questions – the PJIs answer them all.
Nothing is omitted, nothing is left to chance.

During the second week the students are introduced to the aircraft mock-ups. These are exact
representations of Hercules transport aircraft, the
type they will be making their drops from. They
go through all the routines, such as hooking-up
their 'chutes, checking their kit and exit drills.

Exiting an aircraft correctly is crucial. The students are therefore taught how to do it on the exit
trainer. This consists of a tower 22.5m (75ft) high,
from which the men jump. Their harnesses are
connected to a wire, which allows them to
drop as they would if they were making a

Left: Parachute Jump Instructors (PJIs) at Brize Norton check parachutes before a course starts. The PJIs are the best in the world when it comes to teaching men to jump from aircraft. The pre-course checks and assessments they carry out on equipment and training techniques ensure the students get the maximum benefit during their four weeks at the RAF base.

proper jump. As well as giving the men a 'feel' for
a parachute jump, it allows the PJIs to get a look
at how they land. This is where the students first
really appreciate the hours they put in learning
how to land and roll. There are very few injuries
on the exit trainer.

Right: A PJI goes over a jump drill once again for the benefit of a group of students. The PJIs have infinite patience and often explain points over and over again to recruits. They do not mind – they know men's lives are at stake.

During the second week the men are also introduced to the kit they will wear when jumping. This includes their parachutes – the Irwin PX1 Mark 4 main 'chute, worn on the back, and the PR7 reserve, worn on the chest – and their bergens. The bergens are carried under the reserve 'chute when the men exit the aircraft. During the descent they are released and are suspended below each man at the end of a 12m (40ft) line, which is secured to chest webbing by way of two hooks. In this way the bergen hits the ground first, reducing the chances of a landing injury. In addition, there is the soldier's weapon, which is carried in a sleeve on the side of the bergen. The men will also be introduced to the life jackets, which will be worn if they are jumping near water.

The first jump

This familiarisation training takes all of the second week. The third week is when the men make their first jump. Until recently the first jumps were from a balloon. However, as the balloons were made from Indian silk, the Ministry of Defence decided they were too expensive to maintain and scrapped them. Now recruits make their first jump from a Hercules.

The first jump is made without any bergen. The men just wear their main 'chute and reserve. By now they are fully briefed as to procedures. Many are anxious, but an SAS soldier remembers that the jump itself held little fear: 'Of course you're a little apprehensive, but because the training is so good, and you're so used to the word of command, you do everything like clockwork. You have little time to think.'

The SAS recruits file onto the Hercules, along with the other 30 or so students. Each man takes his seat and fastens his seat belt. Some 20 minutes into the flight the order is given to check kit. The men stand up and check their own reserve 'chutes, then check the main 'chute of the man in front.

The command 'action stations' is given, and the men file down the aircraft towards the two doors at the rear of the aircraft, located on each side of the fuselage. They hook up their 'chutes, ready to make their jump in two lines, or 'sticks', one from each door. When they leave the aircraft the lines

Above left and right: Jumping from 1m-high platforms may appear to have little to do with making a parachute jump. However, the students have to learn the correct jump posture and how to land correctly. This is done inside the hangars where the PJIs can monitor each man closely. Only by starting from basics can the instructors guarantee that dangers are reduced a minimum.

will automatically open their parachutes. The doors open, and the first man stands ready, hands grasping each side of the door frame ready to propel him from the aircraft.

The light above each door is red. When the aircraft is over the DZ they change to green. The instructors scream 'go, go, go!' and the men throw themselves out of the aircraft. An SAS soldier remembers his first jump: 'Then you're in the air. You look up and check your 'chute. It's brilliant when the canopy opens and you're descending. You're not worried about the landing. You hit the ground and roll. Elation. You grab your lower rigging lines and pull them to collapse the canopy, otherwise in a high wind you'll get dragged along the ground. It's only after you've made your first jump that you start to worry about landing – because you know what to expect. The landings are definitely worse than the exits.'

The first jump over, the men prepare for drops with bergens. All the jumps are from an altitude of 300m (1000ft). The rest of week three and week four are taken up with the other seven jumps.

The final jump is the night one with full kit. This does cause some jitters, as an SAS soldier explains: 'Even in the Regiment blokes are terrified of parachuting at night, especially the bigger guys. They come down heavier, you see. If they drop you in the wrong place, over power lines and water, you can drown or break your neck. Having said that, at the end of the day it's the coward's option to jump. Does that sound surprising? You have to remember that you are frightened of what people, your mates, are thinking about you. At the end of the day it's easier to jump.'

The night jump over, the SAS men are taken to Hereford, the Regiment's UK base, where they are 'badged'. They are now SAS soldiers.

This sequence shows students on the static-line parachute course, SAS included, making a drop from a Hercules aircraft. The men are equipped with Irvin PX1 Mark 4 main 'chutes and PR7 reserves. The main 'chutes are worn on their backs, with the reserve in front.

1 The command 'action stations' is given and the men stand up to begin their parachute checks.

2 After the checks the men shuffle forward and prepare to jump from the two side doors of the Hercules, which are situated towards the rear of the fuselage.

3 Green light on – GO! The first man is out and the second prepares to follow.

4 The rest of the men throw themselves out of the aircraft, helped on their way by the Parachute Jump Instructors.

5 Outside the aircraft, the main parachutes deploy as the ripcords are automatically pulled by the static lines attached to the inside of the Hercules. The men now prepare to land.

Background picture: Parachutists come into land after making a static-line jump.

GOOD POINTS

✔ The SAS has had only one fatality with regard to parachute courses during its entire 50-year history.

✔ Brize Norton's Parachute Jump Instructors provide the best parachute training in the world.

✔ The overall failure rate on the static-line parachute course at Brize Norton is less than one per cent.

✔ The static-line parachute course is the last hurdle to be passed before a man becomes an SAS man – so very few fail.

BAD POINTS

✘ There is a risk of injuries on the course, especially broken ankles and legs and damaged backs.

✘ Problems in the air are very rare, but any collisions that result in mid-air entanglements are fatal.

✘ Occasionally one parachutist will get underneath another while in the air and 'steal' his air, collapsing the top canopy.

✘ The scrapping of the balloon jump because of cutbacks has taken away a real 'bottle tester' on the course.

ANDY MCNAB
TEAM LEADER

Andy McNab's life story is the stuff of fiction. A teenage tearaway in south London, he later went on to lead the most famous SAS operation of modern times.

Thanks to his book about his exploits during the 1991 Gulf War – *Bravo Two Zero* – Andy McNab (pseudonym) is now one of the most famous SAS soldiers ever to have worn the Winged Dagger badge. His childhood and early Army career suggested anything other than service in the world's crack unit, but his determination ensured he made the grade.

McNab was born in London in 1960. As a baby his natural mother abandoned him in a plastic bag on the steps of Guy's Hospital. He was adopted by a south London couple, and spent a tough childhood and teenage years in Brixton. He was in and out of trouble with the police during this time and narrowly escaped being sent to borstal for burglary. Determined to stay out of trouble in the future, he decided to join the Army. He went along to the recruiting office and failed the academic test. He was told to report a month later, and this time he passed (due to the fact that the test was exactly the same). He ended up at the Infantry Junior Leaders Battalion in Shorncliffe, Kent. From there he went on to the Rifle Depot in Winchester and the Royal Green Jackets.

First blood

By his own admission he was an average soldier. But he liked the Army. It gave him the discipline he had never known and the promise of excitement. He worked hard and his efforts paid off; he was promoted to lance-corporal by the time of his second tour of Northern Ireland in 1979. During the tour his patrol fought off a heavily armed IRA detachment, an event which made him a hero with his regiment.

He was now, in his own words, 'army barmy'. He loved the adrenalin rush of military life. He attained the

How tough do you have to be to be an SAS soldier? Andy McNab poses with the kit he took with him behind the lines in Iraq. He marched and fought carrying a back-breaking load of 95kg (209lb).

Right: *The patrol 'Bravo Two Zero' photographed on the ramp of the Chinook helicopter before their insertion into Iraq during the Gulf War. Patrol members with uncovered faces are those who perished in Iraq. They are, from left to right, Robert Consiglio, 'Legs' Lane and Vince Phillips.*

rank of corporal. It was in 1980, while posted to Tidworth, that he first took an interest in the SAS. He was bored with garrison life. So, yearning for more adventure, he put himself forward for SAS Selection. However, he failed and had to return to the Green Jackets. Undeterred, he applied for the next Selection, which was a winter course. In preparation he trained all through Christmas 1984. This time he succeeded. He passed through all the training, and then received his khaki beret and Winged Dagger badge. He was assigned to Air Troop, B Squadron.

Gulf command

By the time the Gulf War broke out in 1991, he was an SAS sergeant. His patrol, codenamed 'Bravo Two Zero' (the North Road Watch patrol), was sent into Iraq to set up observation posts to watch for enemy Scuds. McNab and his seven comrades found themselves right in the middle of an area of high enemy activity. They set up camp, but were discovered by a young boy tending a herd of goats, who alerted the nearby Iraqi unit. It seemed as though they would all be killed. However, their SAS training stood them in good stead.

There was no other alternative but to flee to the Syrian border, the Iraqis in hot pursuit. The weather at the beginning of 1991 in western Iraq was atrocious. Snow, sleet, rain and freezing temperatures lashed the SAS soldiers. With few rations, inadequate clothing and ever-decreasing supplies of ammunition (there were several battles with Iraqi troops), the odds were against them.

The team was split into small groups by a combination of bad luck and fatigue. The pace was cruel, and very soon it took its toll. Sergeant Vince Phillips got separated and died of hypothermia. Trooper Robert Consiglio was killed by enemy gunfire, while Lance-Corporal 'Legs' Lane also died of hypothermia. Only one of the eight – Corporal Chris Ryan – made it to Syria. The rest, including McNab, were captured.

Cruel capture

Dehydrated, cold and starving, McNab had to endure savage beatings from Iraqi military personnel as they tried to make him 'confess' to being Israeli. However, his SAS training carried him through this ordeal. No matter how badly he was beaten, he kept his mind working. He tried to think up ways of appeasing his interrogators without giving them any information. These sessions dislocated his shoulder, reduced his face to a bloody mess and ruptured several muscles in his back. The Iraqis forced him to eat his own excrement, which gave him hepatitis. But he did not give in.

He was awarded the Military Medal after the war – a just reward for a true SAS hero. He retired from the Regiment in 1993 and wrote *Bravo Two Zero* about his Gulf War experiences. He now lives abroad.

BACKGROUND

Andy McNab is not the first SAS soldier to write about his service in the Regiment, and now there is a booming industry concerning ex-SAS members committing their memoirs to print. This trend is viewed with some alarm by the Regiment itself, which as a unit operates in the shadows, well away from the media spotlight. In addition, the British Ministry of Defence, which is concerned about secrets being made public, is also concerned about ex-SAS soldiers putting pen to paper. Ex-SAS men themselves are naturally keen to tell their stories, such as Soldier 'I', not least to earn the kind of money that McNab himself has amassed. The publication of *Storm Command* and *Looking for Trouble*, both written by General de la Billière, a former SAS soldier himself, has increased the determination of serving and ex-SAS soldiers to get a 'slice of the action' and reveal the true face of the SAS. Chris Ryan, for example, a member of 'Bravo Two Zero', has written his own account of the mission entitled *The One That Got Away*.

ANDY McNAB
DCM MM
BRAVO TWO ZERO
The True Story of an SAS Patrol behind the lines in Iraq

CHRIS RYAN

AGAINST ALL ODDS

Even by the SAS's standards Chris Ryan is something special, among the best of the best. His epic solo trek to freedom has made him a legend at Stirling Lines.

The philosophy of the SAS is 'train hard, fight easy', and there can be no better example of the tough training instilled in its soldiers than in the extraordinary story of Corporal Chris Ryan, B Squadron, 22 SAS.

The SAS mission tasked to the patrol codenamed 'Bravo Two Zero' during the 1991 Gulf War is without doubt one of the most famous stories of 'behind-the-lines' actions in modern warfare. Ambushed by Iraqi troops and savaged by the viciously cold weather, the eight-man patrol ditched their bergens and fled on foot to the Syrian border. Behind them the countryside was alive with the enemy.

Flight

SAS soldiers remain cool under fire. As Ryan grabbed a 66mm rocket launcher, he remembered his hip flask in his bergen. It had been a Christmas present from his wife. It would take more than a few Iraqis to make him leave it behind. He raced back to his pack and found it, all the time enemy rounds pumping into the ground around him.

The SAS soldiers headed west. During their flight they got separated, until Ryan was on his own. He didn't give up – SAS soldiers never give up. He did the only logical thing: he carried on walking.

Ryan had little food and water on him, and what he did have was soon used up. By the third day he was mentally and physically shattered. Most ordinary soldiers would have given up. However, SAS troops are not ordinary. Ryan carried on. He told his mind he did not need food. Very soon his boots were cut to ribbons, and his feet were bleeding. He carried on.

Triumph in the face of adversity

By the sixth day he was severely dehydrated. He needed water fast. He then came across a stream. He drank greedily from it. Unfortunately it was full of waste from a uranium processing plant farther upstream. He developed blood and liver problems as a result. He carried on. After seven nights and eight days alone, he reached the Syrian border and safety. He had walked a total of 300km (225 miles).

His journey was a supreme example of what makes an SAS soldier tick. The gruelling endurance marches on Selection and afterwards prepared Ryan physically for his trial in Iraq. But it was his mental toughness that saw him through.

Ryan was born just outside Newcastle in 1961. A fanatical climbing enthusiast, he was, even by the Regiment's standards, reckoned to be super-fit. He left the SAS in 1994 and wrote *The One That Got Away* about his Gulf War experiences. He now lives in the south of England.

Left: Most of the Iraqis who had this view of Chris Ryan ended up dead.
Below: Ryan and the rest of 'Bravo Two Zero' were transported behind the lines in Iraq in CH-47 Chinook helicopters such as this one. However, they had to try and get back to base on foot.
Right: Iraqi troops like these failed to capture Ryan during his flight.

BACKGROUND

Chris Ryan's valour in the 1991 Gulf War won him the Military Medal. Though he made a full recovery from his physical injuries, it was the mental damage that was the most enduring. The mission in Iraq affected Ryan psychologically, and at one point he showed signs of Post-Traumatic Stress Disorder, an illness which the Ministry of Defence does not recognise. He suffered flashbacks and became distant from his wife. This put a strain on his marriage. Fortunately, with help, he was able to sort himself out, and he and his wife and child are now back together. Some wounds take longer to heal than others.

DAVID STIRLING
FATHER OF THE SAS

The genius and determination of David Stirling led to the creation of the world's most famous elite unit, and the principles he laid down for the SAS endure to this day.

The founder of the Special Air Service was born in 1915. The descendant of a long line of Scottish gentry, the 'boy David' spent his childhood in Scotland before being educated at Ampleforth College and Cambridge University. Although he read architecture at university, Stirling had a love of the outdoor life, especially hunting and mountaineering. When World War II broke out in 1939, for example, he was in the USA training for a climb of Mount Everest.

When he heard about the outbreak of the war the lanky (he was 1.95m [6.5ft] tall) Scot travelled back to Britain and enlisted in the Scots Guards. He soon got bored, though, and so volunteered for one of the new Commandos that were being formed. He joined No 8 Commando, which was commanded by Captain Robert Laycock. The new unit was then sent to the Middle East as Layforce (Laycock had been promoted to brigadier and his unit had been expanded to three Commandos).

The SAS is born

Stirling witnessed some ineffectual large-scale British Commando raids on the North African coastline, and came to the conclusion that a number of small-scale units launched against the enemy on the same night would be much more effective. These ideas remained in Stirling's mind until he was involved in a parachute accident that put him in hospital. While he was recovering he put his ideas down on paper. He believed that 200 men split into five-man teams could achieve results out of all proportion to their size if they were used correctly. He bluffed his way into Middle East Headquarters and handed his notes to the Deputy Chief of Staff, General Neil Ritchie, who read them and agreed to pass them on.

As a consequence of his audacity, Stirling was promoted to captain and authorised to raise his unit – the SAS was born. It was one of Stirling's great talents that he was able to spot and enlist men of the right calibre into his unit. Very soon the SAS was filled with individuals of vision and charisma who were ideally suited to lead troops in the type of operations behind enemy lines that he had in mind: 'Paddy' Mayne, Johnny Cooper, 'Jock' Lewes and Reg Seeking.

Triumph and disaster

After a shaky start the SAS started to achieve spectacular results. Stirling himself took an active part in missions against Axis airfields and other targets throughout 1941-42. By the beginning of 1943 he had under his command 1 SAS, a Greek squadron, a Special Boat Section, a French squadron and the Special Interrogation Group, in all 700 men.

The future of the SAS looked assured, but Stirling's was not as bright. On 22 January 1943, while operating with five Jeeps near the Gabes Gap in Tunisia, his group was surrounded by Germans and captured.

Above left: David Stirling, the founder of the SAS.
Left: Stirling with an SAS jeep patrol in North Africa in 1942.
He saw the wisdom of using small groups of highly mobile teams to strike at the enemy behind the lines, as opposed to the large-scale Commando raids that had been previously used.

BACKGROUND

The Commandos were formed by the British as a way of hitting back against Nazi-occupied Europe. Their name came from the Boer irregulars who fought the British at the turn of the century. The idea was to combine guerrilla-like resources and independence with military professionalism. Churchill himself was very enthusiastic. It was against this background that men such as Stirling were able to turn their ideas into reality, as the British High Command was willing to listen to anyone with plans about how to hit the enemy using as few resources as possible.

Stirling himself, nicknamed the 'Phantom Major' by the enemy because of his unit's elusiveness, was at first taken to an Italian prison camp at Gavi. However, following four escapes from there he was taken to Colditz, where he remained until the war's end. Though his part in hostilities had ended, his vision and drive had ensured that the SAS would survive, and the guiding principles he established for the Regiment have remained unchanged. He died in 1990.

Left: Colditz Castle, where David Stirling was held prisoner from August 1944 after his capture in North Africa and a number of escapes from Italian prisoner-of-war camps. Stirling quite liked Colditz, as he himself wrote: 'The company was good and the food very palatable.'

PETER DE LA BILLIÈRE
THE QUIET SOLDIER

Sir Peter de la Billière is one of the most famous SAS soldiers of the modern era. A rather undisciplined individual during his early life, like many men he found the informal yet exciting regime of the SAS to be suited to his personality. His career with the SAS took him to the deserts of the Middle East, the jungles of the Far East and on to high command.

Peter de la Billière was born in 1934. His father was a naval surgeon, though Peter did not see much of him. He was away at sea most of the time during his early childhood, and he was killed when his ship was torpedoed by German bombers in 1941.

The young Peter was sent to Harrow School, but the formal environment did not curb his rebellious spirit. Probably the lack of a father figure was responsible for his attitude. On one occasion, for example, he stole a rifle from the school's armoury and sniped at a room containing several of his fellow pupils!

The appeal of the SAS

By his own admission he was poor academically, but his fortunes improved somewhat when he joined the Army. He was commissioned into the Durham Light Infantry and served in the Korean War, but early on he had decided he wanted to join the SAS. His reasons give an insight into his mind, as well as that of a typical SAS soldier: 'What appealed to me about the SAS was the fact that it operated in small groups behind enemy lines: its soldiers were left on their own for months on end, and had to be able to live with themselves, rather than as part of a structured group.'

He joined the Regiment as a captain in Malaya in 1955, in time to fight communist terrorists in the humid jungles of the Far East. Next stop was northern Oman. He took part in the SAS campaign against the rebels holding out on the Jebel Akhdar (Green Mountain), which won him the Military Cross. At that time he was only 24 years old.

To be an SAS soldier a man must also have an enquiring mind, and so it was with de la Billière. In the winter of 1963-64 he served with the Federal Regular Army in Aden, and later went on to command A Squadron, 22 SAS. He established a close-quarter battle course for SAS soldiers in Aden, and laid the basis for the Regiment's counter-terrorist tactics.

His next deployment was to Borneo, where he undertook a thorough reorganisation of the SAS. He won a second Military Cross. Service in Oman in the 1970s resulted in him winning the Distinguished Service Order, and by the end of the decade

Above: Peter de la Billière as a lieutenant-general in the 1991 Gulf War. His hands-on approach went down well with the 35,000 people serving under him, and he got on well with Schwarzkopf, the command-in-chief. Right: Part of de la Billière's Gulf command – 1st Armoured Division.

he led the SAS Group. His efforts in the post turned the Regiment into the world's crack anti-terrorist unit, which was just as well, for it was well placed to deal with the Iranian Embassy siege in May 1980. The success of the assault to free the hostages propelled the SAS into the media spotlight. But, like all SAS soldiers, de la Billière kept his feet firmly on the ground: 'In the Regiment we never felt that we had any cause to be complacent.'

By the time of the Falklands War in 1982 de la Billière was a brigadier, and it was his influence that ensured the SAS went south with the British Task Force. After commanding British forces in the 1991 Gulf War he was awarded a knighthood and promoted to general before retiring from active service.

It is said in many Army circles that a career in the SAS can make promotion outside the Regiment difficult, if not impossible. However, the career of Peter de la Billière has shown that it is possible to achieve high rank after wearing the SAS beret and Winged Dagger badge. During the 1991 Gulf War, for example, he was the commander of the British forces sent to Arabia. And he is not the first SAS soldier to achieve high command: both Johnny Watts and Tony Jeapes finished their Army careers with the rank of major-general after SAS service.

TONY JEAPES
TURNING VISIONS INTO REALITY

Tony Jeapes was an SAS officer whose vision and inspired leadership during the Regiment's war in Oman in the 1970s made a major contribution to eventual victory. He eventually rose to become the commander of 22 SAS itself.

Above: Tony Jeapes, here wearing the uniform of a major-general as the commander of South West District, UK Land Forces. He wrote a book about his Omani experiences entitled SAS Operation Oman.

Being an elite soldier often means more than merely being able to fight well, important though this undoubtedly is. In the SAS, a soldier, especially an officer, must have vision, that ill-defined quality that allows him to rise above the mundane and take a wider perspective. Tony Jeapes was such a man, and his leadership of SAS units during the Regiment's war in Oman (1970-76) contributed to a great victory.

Tony Jeapes was originally a member of the Dorset Regiment, but he decided the SAS was for him – he joined the elite as a lieutenant in 1958. He soon showed himself to be a man of action. In January 1959, for example, he took part in the Jebel Akhdar cam-

paign in northern Oman. A group of rebels were ensconced on the Jebel Akhdar (the Green Mountain) and the Sultan's forces were unable to dislodge them. The British Government, having a treaty of friendship with Oman, subsequently sent military aid, which included the SAS.

The culmination of the campaign was a daring assault by the SAS units up the almost sheer rocky slopes of the mountain. Lieutenant Jeapes was with A Squadron, and was soon engaged in savage fighting with the enemy. But the SAS had the initiative and the rebels were defeated. For his part in the action he was awarded the Military Cross.

Jeapes in Dhofar

But it was the next war in Oman, in the south of the country, which would show Jeapes' true talents. In January 1971, Major Jeapes was sent to Dhofar Province in southern Oman. Once again the British had been called upon to support the Sultan, this time in his war against Dhofari insurgents, and once again the Special Air Service was despatched.

Many SAS officers had immediately recognised the main problem in Dhofar: the Sultan's repressive measures, backed up by the heavy-handedness of the Sultan's Armed Forces (SAF) were forcing the locals into the hands of the rebels. The commander of the Regiment at that time, Lieutenant-Colonel Johnny Watts, devised a counter-insurgency programme for winning the locals over the Sultan's cause, called the 'five fronts campaign'.

Setting up the *firqat* units

As Jeapes himself wrote: 'It was first and last a war about people, a war in which both sides concentrated upon winning the support of civilians of the Jebel Dhofar and which was won in the end by civil development, with military action merely a means to that end.' As well as the civil aid programme, Jeapes was also instrumental in establishing the *firqat* units (Dhofari irregulars trained by the SAS). Together with Salim Mubarak, a former rebel, he helped set up the first *firqat* unit, *Firqat Salahadin*. As more *firqat* units were formed, Jeapes was the key figure in ensuring that SAS, SAF and *firqats* cooperated with each other. This was no easy task, for many in the SAF, especially the officers, thought *firqat* personnel were untrustworthy at best and outright bandits at worst. Nevertheless, Jeapes and the SAS persevered, and gradually a working relationship did develop between the the Sultan's troops and the *firqat* units, although it was never completely harmonious.

The seeds of victory

By the time Jeapes and his A Squadron left Dhofar in May 1971 a start had been made: the SAS had led several offensives against rebel positions on the Jebel Dhofar, and the Omani Government had established a presence in territory hitherto enemy held. More importantly, there were several hundred Dhofaris fighting in *firqats* and the civil aid programme was in full swing.

Jeapes returned to Oman during the next five years of the war, by which time it had been won. He himself continued his career rise. By 1974 he was the commander of the Regiment itself, leading it on active duty in both Oman and Northern Ireland. Colonel Jeapes was awarded the OBE in 1977, and taught counter-insurgency tactics at the British Army's Staff College. He retired from active service holding the rank of major-general.

In the early 1980s he wrote a book about his Oman experiences entitled SAS *Operation Oman*.

Left: SAF soldiers during the war in southern Oman in the early 1970s. Jeapes helped SAF/firqat relations during the conflict, though many of the Sultan's officers remained highly suspicious of their firqat comrades, regarding them as ill-disciplined.